VISUAL
RESEARCH

Fairchild Books

An imprint of Bloomsbury Publishing Plc
Imprint previously known as AVA Publishing

50 Bedford Square	1385 Broadway
London	New York
WC1B 3DP	NY 10018
UK	USA

www.bloomsbury.com

FAIRCHILD BOOKS, BLOOMSBURY and the Diana logo are trademarks of Bloomsbury Publishing Plc

British Library Cataloguing-in-Publication Data
A catalogue record for this book is available from the British Library.
ISBN: PB: 978-1-4742-3290-6
           ePDF: 978-1-4742-3291-3

Library of Congress Cataloging-in-Publication Data
Bestley, Russell, author.
Visual Research: An Introduction to Research Methods in Graphic Design—
Third Edition.
Includes bibliographical references and index.
ISBN: 978-1-4742-3290-6 (PB)
           978-1-4742-3291-3 (ePDF)
1. Graphic arts—Research. 2. Design—Research. I.
Noble, Ian, 1960—author. II. Title.
NC997.B44 2016   745.4072'1—dc23   2015020465

Series: Required Reading Range

Design by Russell Bestley

Printed and bound in China

VISUAL RESEARCH

AN INTRODUCTION TO RESEARCH METHODS IN GRAPHIC DESIGN

IAN NOBLE AND RUSSELL BESTLEY

3rd Edition

Fairchild Books

An imprint of Bloomsbury Publishing Plc

B L O O M S B U R Y

LONDON · OXFORD · NEW YORK · NEW DELHI · SYDNEY

Table of Contents

Foreword

We tend to think of graphic design in terms of finished goods: a neatly polished poster, logo, layout, or Web site. Yet graphic design is also a process. A designed artifact emerges from a set of questions whose answers often bump around in the dark before a solution bubbles up to the surface.

Think of this book as a series of answers to questions you may have about graphic design. The questions are posed through concrete examples of work, reproduced with enough depth and scale to let you come safely inside. This is a big book, not because it has to look good on your coffee table but because the ideas are big. The pages have opened their arms wide to make a comfortable place for reading and thinking.

What is research? Research is about looking for something in a focused and systematic way. Scientists and scholars study the published literature and proven results on a topic that they seek to explore; they also set out to create new knowledge through active experimentation. The subject of this book is visual research: the emphasis is on making and doing, not reading and writing. Design itself is a form of research, following both measured and intuitive sequences of investigation in order to arrive at new forms and insights.

First published in 2005, *Visual Research* is an invaluable tool for designers and educators. This new edition revisits classic project prompts and provides updated case studies and fresh commentary by design professionals. A new chapter, "Visual Research Analytical Tools," invites designers to discover patterns in the world around them through qualitative and quantitative analysis.

Does methodology matter? Graphic design is a creative field, not a science. A designer's process tends to be more loopy than linear, tracking back and forth rather than pushing stalwartly forward. Embracing a method, trying it on for size, can help designers shake up their personal habits and dig up fresh results. Pursuing a more structured path can take you to unexpected places. You will find in this book new vocabularies for asking what signs, materials, and images can mean. Rhetoric and semiotics offer ways to consider design's linguistic and social contexts. Mapping and data visualization provide logical means for organizing information and displaying it in illuminating ways. The systematic analysis of a written text can generate richly textured typographies.

This book presents theory as a tool for both synthesis and analysis. The ultimate goal of visual research is to inform form, to infuse signs and surfaces with meaning. A designer is a creative intellectual who makes systems and things, studying the world of objects, users, and information in order to create living acts of communication. The tools and methods laid out in this book provide a helpful introduction to the methodologies of creative thinking.

Ellen Lupton
Graphic designer, writer, curator and educator

Introduction

The title of this book—*Visual Research*—describes the fundamental process of systematic inquiry within graphic design. Research in the context of graphic design practice can be seen as an underpinning and defining activity, based on the notions of *problem solving* and employing a combination of theoretical and visual tools and methods as part of the iterative—step-by-step—nature of the design process. For many designers, research is a necessary activity in exploring how best to arrive at a meaningful and effective solution to the needs of a client and the demands of a brief. The many factors at work can range from the prosaic and pragmatic to the sophisticated and poetic. This comprehension, born of training, experience, practical skill, and personal philosophy, defines the designer and his or her personal and idiosyncratic methods of working.

For other designers, visual research may be more related to design as a *problem-finding* activity: a practice based not on the search for definitive answers to specific questions but on a critical approach to interrogating and understanding the world around us. In this instance, the research activity is focused on the quality and manner of how the questions are asked. In this context, research is not only a rational or deductive working process; it can also be considered an outcome in its own right, framing the inquiry and offering the viewer or reader a further insight into the subject at hand. The designer may begin with a loosely formed question based on prior knowledge and experience of a subject, and through his or her research, may arrive at what might be called a better question, rather than an answer. Documentation and critique of the journey traveled can be of significance not only to the designer but also to others with an interest in the field, and can

help shape and progress our collective knowledge and understanding.

These descriptions of design research should not be seen as an indication of a distinction between pure and applied research, or as a suggestion that a hierarchy of significance or importance can be placed on either way of working. They are both a significant part of what we might consider contemporary visual communication design and the wide-ranging approaches to the discipline that currently exist. This book is an attempt to map the field of visual research within the practice of graphic design and to offer an introduction to the research methods and models that have formed the basis of our teaching over the last fifteen years. Recognition of this reflective aspect of design is long overdue, particularly when education and cultural institutions have a long history of critical engagement within parallel disciplines in the creative industries. As Rick Poynor noted in 2011:

> *For anyone located within design, visual studies' failure to acknowledge and address the central role of graphic design as a shaper of the visual environment, alongside the forms of visual culture that it does acknowledge – art, film, television, photography, advertising, new media – must seem unaccountable. What could explain this peculiar blindness among a group of academics hyper-attuned to most forms of visuality?*[1]

The Bigger Picture
The various chapters in this book explore the many aspects of visual research from the perspective of both practice and theory, and they are supported throughout with practical examples of projects that illustrate the ideas and processes discussed. The work featured in the

Introduction

case studies in this new edition was created by some of the students with whom we have worked over recent years. We also revisit some projects featured in previous volumes of *Visual Research*, charting the ways in which the methods employed at the time then matured and developed within the subsequent professional lives of the designers involved. This book and the programs of study that these students undertook are a product of one another. All designers were encouraged to explore their individual understanding of the role of research within their working methods and the work that they produced. In turn, their ideas fed our own understanding of how to develop a meaningful approach to the teaching of graphic design as a critical, research-based activity.

This new edition of *Visual Research* features a new chapter on *Tools for Visual Analysis*, twelve case studies, and updated and revised chapters, exercises, and glossary. Our approach to the subject of visual research has grown and developed since the first edition, and this updated version of the book represents the further refinement of a key set of methodologies that can be used by graphic designers and visual communicators in the development of clear, purposeful, and strategic design solutions.

Designing Design Research

The verb *to design* literally means to plan something for a specific role, purpose, or effect. As a noun, *design* can be defined as an act of creative reasoning—a process

whereby the designer balances lateral, original thinking with pragmatic, logical, solution-driven methods. The act of *designing*, in terms of visual communication and graphic design, centers on the ways in which a designer addresses practical and theoretical problems through a broad range of often two-dimensional (print-based), but increasingly also three-dimensional or time-based, media, materials, and processes.

What has become evident over recent years is that while the social, cultural, and technological context that graphic design exists within is subject to an ever-accelerating rate of change and flux, the key attributes needed in order to function as a designer have remained broadly consistent. These skills are directly related to visual research: methods of working and patterns of inquiry based on what could be called sustainable thinking. This mode of engagement provides a significant focus on what the designer and educator Jan van Toorn has described as "the designer's field of operation." In practice, this is an informed and critical approach to design practice based on rigorous models of exploration and testing that inform both the formal and cultural aspects of the designer's role.

Three useful models of graphic design research are adapted in this book from Christopher Frayling's research approaches and definitions, based on the methodologies, processes, initial aims, and final objectives of a design investigation, published in his work *Research in Art and Design* (1994). Frayling's model is adapted somewhat here,

Logic
An iterative and reasoned process of human thought that involves the interrogation of a problem, or the creation of a solution to a problem, in a linear, step-by-step manner.

Creativity
Creativity is a mental process involving the discovery of new and innovative ideas or concepts, or new associations between existing ideas or concepts. Creative processes may also lead

to extensions and adaptations of existing concepts and theories in an original and previously unexplored manner.

in order to present a clear distinction among different areas of graphic design research and practice. Models of design research are based on the following themes:

Research about Design. The study of design histories, styles, influences, models, and approaches. The main objective is to understand a context or history from different perspectives, such as design criticism and historical research. The goal is related to the deduction of new knowledge and understanding of design as a subject.

Research into Design. The exploration of design methods and practices, including visual testing and experimentation. This research is centered on both understanding the process of design and developing new design actions, artifacts, or methods.

Research through Design. The use of graphic design as an instrument for investigating and articulating a particular subject area that lies outside of the field of design—as such, this model of design research would include mapping, information design, and editorial approaches to visualizing and categorizing data.

The Structure of the Book
Visual Research is divided into thematic chapters exploring several different emphases in relation to research-based graphic design. The case studies reflect a range of practical responses to the themes explored, from visual grammar and design literacy to the relationship between audience and message and the investigation of materials and processes. The book also includes a series of design exercises, enabling readers to reflect on the content explored and to further their

own understanding of the discipline. Key concepts outline ideas and theories that can inform the design process, together with examples of the application of those theories from the perspective of the graphic design practitioner: it is important to reflect on how ideas might be applied and may be of use to designers in their practice—in the actual *making* of graphic design. As design writer and practitioner Andrew Howard notes,

> *Visual communication is not simply dependent on the power of thought. It is a process of making—of transforming ideas into tangible expressions. Thinking and making are not alternatives to each other. They are forces of reciprocal power within the design process. One cannot take place without the other.*[2]

Visual Research provides several graphic devices to aid reader navigation. Running headlines give a clear indication of each section of the book: chapters, case studies, key concepts, and exercises. Color coding of pages for key concepts and exercises helps delineate those sections, while running glossaries and image captions are also differentiated typographically.

There is not sufficient space available to give credit to the many people who have contributed to our understanding of the subject of this book, but it is important to thank the designers who have given their time and energy in providing the work featured here. This book is the product of many years of collaboration, reflection, and debate among graphic design educators, students, and professionals. We hope that the debate will continue.

1. "Out of the Studio: Graphic Design History and Visual Studies," *Design Observer*, 2011.
2. "A Manifesto for Higher Learning," *Design Observer*, 2013.

CHAPTER 01
WHY AND HOW?
THE ROLE OF RESEARCH IN GRAPHIC DESIGN: SEMIOTICS, ANALYSIS, COMMUNICATION THEORY, SYSTEMATIC APPROACHES, SEMANTICS, AND DISCOURSE THEORY

Research Methodologies

This book provides an introduction to a range of research methods for graphic designers. This important aspect of graphic design practice encompasses a wide range of practical and theoretical applications, and this chapter introduces the field of research methodology as both an analytical and a practical tool for graphic designers. By investigating these twin areas of research in parallel, we aim to establish the role of critical thinking as a support to the development of what can be described as an *engaged* form of design practice. Research is an intrinsic aspect of graphic design practice and an essential part of the activity of problem solving. The designer is involved in a constant process of inquiry. It could be said that this process is predicated upon the notion of questioning—whether that leads to a discrete outcome or solution, such as an industrial prototype based on a client's needs, or whether it contributes to the discourse and debate in the form of a proposition or a further question.

Primary theoretical models of design analysis and visual research will also be introduced, including semiotics, communication theory, systematic approaches to design problem solving, semantics, the role of experimentation and play, rhetoric and discourse theory, as well as secondary research models and the testing of ideas and methods. The underlying emphasis throughout this book is on why we do what we do and how, through testing, feedback, and rigorous approaches, we can be sure it is effective in the process of visual communication.

Problematizing Design

The discipline of graphic design can be defined in a variety of ways. The most persistent definition over its relatively short history has described it as a problem-solving activity. This phrase, something of a mantra for a large section of the design community, has been employed to describe the function of graphic design in a commercial sense. It is a sound bite that can be understood by the commissioners of designers—the clients. The client presents the designer with a practical problem that needs to be addressed, the designer then acts to find ways to solve that problem, employing a form of applied research, and the client pays the designer for his or her expertise. This definition has not only legitimized the business and commercial aspects of design but has also led to a restricted description of the function of graphic design that often excludes what might be considered as its wider social, educational, and informational roles.

A broader interpretation could characterize it as a process of analysis and synthesis. Analysis relates to the methods of investigation, inquiry, and understanding that are central to the research of a project brief, concept, or a particular context. Synthesis, meanwhile, is the means by which a designer is able to draw on his or her analytical work and investigation to produce meaningful solutions or interventions. This ability is based on the individual designer's intentions and understanding of a complex range of interrelated issues affecting the creation of a successful

Method
A way of proceeding or doing something, especially in a systematic or regular manner; an action or system of actions toward a goal.

Methodology
A body or collection of methods employed in a particular activity.

Pure Research
The investigation of graphic and visual languages in a propositional sense, rather than those that have a predetermined commercial application.

Applied Research
The investigation of a practical problem, usually with the underlying intention of creating potential practical solutions.

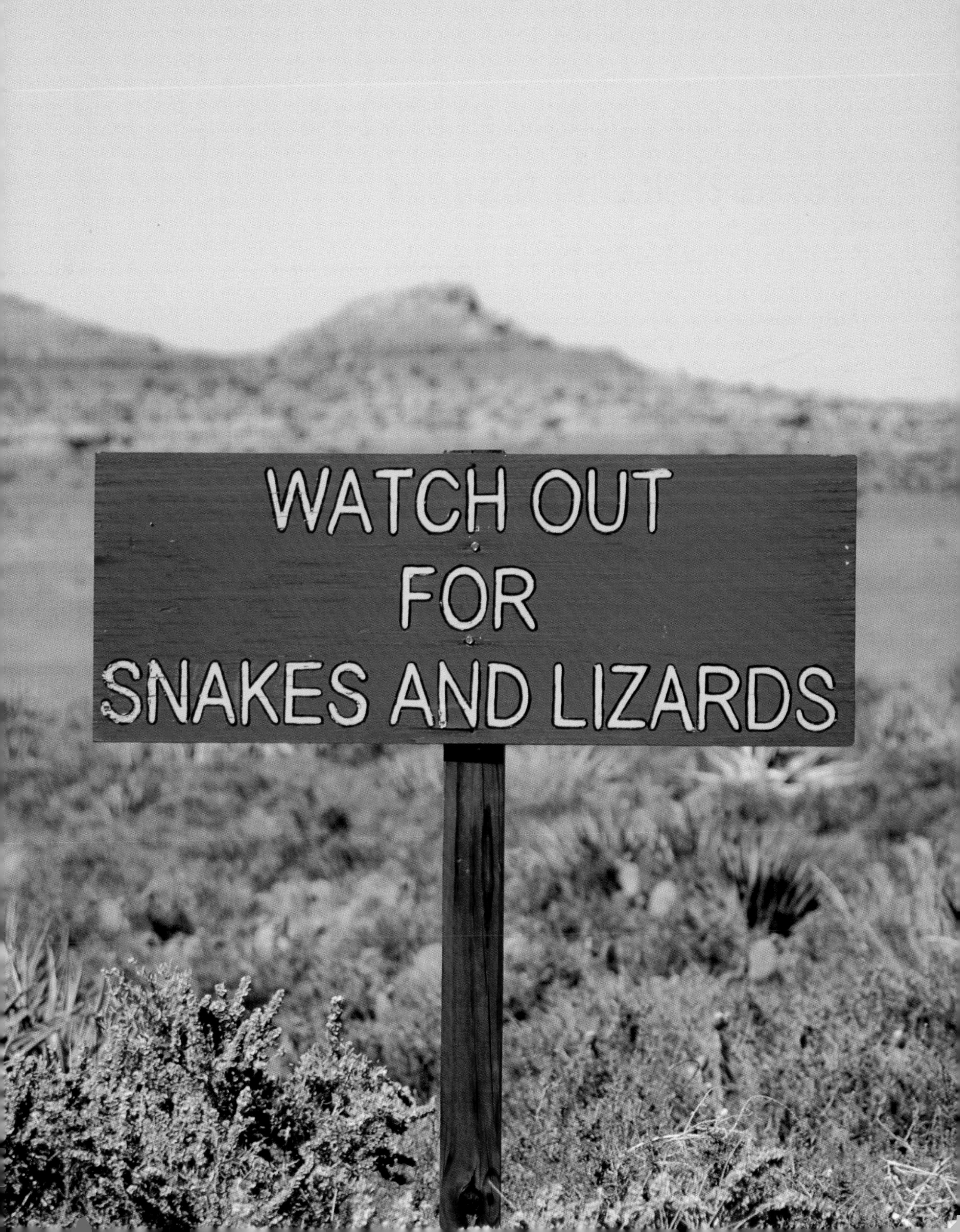
WATCH OUT
FOR
SNAKES AND LIZARDS

Research Methodologies

graphic solution: audience, message or product, budget, materials, the means of production, the employment of an appropriate visual language, and the final form the outcome will take.

Design Research

Can be defined as critical investigation, a search or inquiry to discover new facts and information, or the collection and collation of old data in order to evaluate and test hypotheses or design proposals. This would encompass the study of a subject, employing the analysis of quantitative and/or qualitative data. Research employs methods and schemes of testing to interpret events, facts, or information, and it is a process of observation, discovery, and recording. In the context of graphic design, research provides the foundations of the design process of problem solving and visual communication. The research component of a graphic design brief can take a singular form in some projects, such as the collation of audience feedback to a proposal, or it can operate in several forms simultaneously, each body of research findings working together and in tandem to inform the overall approach to a project.

> *"Research" could mean different things. It could mean research "for" design and research "by" design … Research "by" design means that the process itself is a type of research.*
> Metahaven, *On Design and Research*, Iaspis Forum on Design and Critical Practice, 2009.

In recent years, graphic design has grown to accommodate a wide variety of approaches and intentions. Significantly, for some designers, research is a central and defining activity in their work. In these cases, research is more than an activity used to define effective visual solutions to a client's brief or design problem. It instead becomes an outcome in its own right, informing a designer's or design group's approach, and it generates a way of developing new ideas and techniques of thinking and making. Although this form of research may not lead to real-world practical solutions, this does not obviate the need for a thorough analysis of the context of the work in relation to the potential audience and the stated project intentions. The outcomes of pure research are propositional and offer potential visual solutions to as-yet-undefined questions; in some cases, they define the problem yet to be solved. The act of designing can in itself then lead to new discoveries and insights into the subject under investigation.

> *There can be a discipline of design, but it must be different in kind from disciplines which possess determinate subject matters. Design is a discipline where the conception of subject matter, method, and purpose is an integrated part of the activity and of the results … not products, as such, but the art of conceiving and planning products.*
> Richard Buchanan, "Rhetoric, Humanism and Design," in *Discovering Design: Explorations in Design Studies* (1995).

Terms of Reference

Design research is both guided by and forms the underpinning rationale for the development of a theory of design. A theory is a comprehensive and explanatory framework or system of concepts; it is a set of rules or procedures formulated in the mind. In this instance, it is a way to think about, describe, analyze, and propose design approaches and solutions. A theoretical model or plan can generate several hypotheses, which are assumptions or suggested explanations for a group of facts or phenomena that are used as a basis for further investigation and verification, or are accepted as likely to be true in the case of a *working hypothesis*. A hypothesis is a specific prediction or supposition, typically derived from a theory, which the researcher can use as a basis for testing, benchmarking, or as a model to react against in the formulation of alternative strategies or practices.

> *The idea that a designer was an artiste first and a communicator second (or third) was quaint at the outset but has offered diminished returns over the long term. Although individual personality routinely plays a key role in visual communication, it must be the result, not the goal, of solving design problems.*
> Steven Heller, "The Me Too Generation," in *The Graphic Design Reader* (2002).

Many strategies can be applied to this basic framework for research in graphic design, and they bring with them specific terms that are useful to the designer in describing what is taking place in the staging of a graphic design project. Many of these terms are drawn from outside the field of graphic design and are borrowed from allied or tangential disciplines that have a long tradition of reflection and debate. Subjects such as linguistics, communication studies, art history, philosophy, and the social sciences, for example, have provided useful terms and definitions that designers have been able to adapt and employ in the foundation of a more descriptive language for the processes at work within the creation of visual solutions.

This is not to suggest that visual communication lacks its own specific language. The designer and historian Richard Hollis has described graphic design as constituting a language in its own right: "a language with an uncertain grammar and a continuously expanding vocabulary."[1] Like many activities with a background and history in the technological arena, designers have developed a wide range of terms to describe what is at work in the production of visual communication. Much of this terminology is rooted in the pragmatic description of technical issues, such as color and type specification, information hierarchy, and printing processes, or is influenced by the now commonplace computer and software language (e.g., terms such as file format, resolution, and page layout). It is interesting to also note how some of these terms have migrated into our wider language and common vernacular, largely as a result of increasing public familiarity with desktop publishing and social media. Descriptions of typeface, font name, size or style, image resolution, or format and screen conventions are widely used, if not always fully understood.

The most recent, and probably the most significant, development for contemporary graphic designers came with the arrival of the Apple Macintosh computer (introduced in 1984), along with subsequent developments in desktop publishing technologies across various operating platforms, bringing with it a new language related to design. At the same time, this advance made obsolete many of the traditional processes used by graphic designers, which related to an earlier age of mechanical, rather than digital, reproduction—though, rather ironically, many of the terms associated with that earlier era were adopted (or adapted) within the new media. The debate surrounding the impact and value of

Research Methodologies

this particular technology continues today, more than 30 years after its initial introduction.

The computer has indisputably altered the landscape of graphic design, allowing designers to function in a way that was not previously possible and offering new creative opportunities with greater levels of control over a range of production processes. Designers have acquired more control over the development of their work, but this control has brought with it more responsibility and, some would argue, a loss of specialist knowledge and expertise. We have also witnessed a belated resurgence in interest in analog and more traditional processes, such as letterpress, printmaking, signwriting, and book design, in part because of a perceived homogenization of design aesthetics brought about by desktop publishing and the widespread adoption of standard software packages. Equally, as a work platform, the computer has been influential in opening up new opportunities for designers, while also acting as a catalyst for much of the new debate within the profession—for instance those surrounding notions of authorship, audience, and legibility—and has encouraged designers to explore new roles.

Thinking Differently

The South American design educator and writer Jorge Frascara has written that "the design of the design method and the design of the research method are tasks of a higher order than the design of the communications."[2]

This statement identifies a key shift in design thinking in recent years. The expanding definition of what might be considered the practice of graphic design has been influenced by factors other than technology. The speculative and more experimental work at the margins of contemporary graphic design, an area that could be termed the avant-garde, together with a range of self-authored graphic projects produced by designers working to their own brief, has also exerted a strong influence.

These initiatives often offer new visual grammars and graphic forms, and they can focus on areas of graphic design that were previously constrained and underexamined by a singular, commercially focused definition of the discipline. This more recent concentration on the processes and methods involved in graphic design—a conscious reflection on the *how* and the *why* of the practice—has allowed the area of research methodologies to take on a greater degree of significance to the subject. The discussion of graphic design in university design departments, art colleges, and design journals now routinely includes reference to a diverse set of issues that include the designer's responsibilities in a social, cultural, and economic sense, the role of the designer in communicating to audiences, and the construction of meaning in verbal and visual languages. This wider field of operation has increased the exploration of the processes at work and has broadened the scope of research in graphic design as a subset of

Deductive Research
Research that starts from the position of a general conclusion and then searches for data to support it.

Empirical Research
Investigation into a field of study that is based on direct observation of phenomena.

visual communication or communication design, both within the academies and the professional arena.

For a long period during the development of the discipline, the discussion of graphic design as an activity and its place in the wider community was left to external voices—those who received or observed design, rather than those who created it. Although this provided a useful tool for understanding graphic design, very few of these voices were heard from within the practice itself. Journalists, historians, and cultural theorists who have written about graphic design have usually done so in terms of the artifact or end product and its effect in a social or cultural context. With very few exceptions, the process of design problem solving, the methodologies employed by designers, and their intentions and conceptual approaches to the *practice* of graphic design were left underexplored. Meanwhile, commentary from within the profession was long centered on commercial portfolio reviews, award-winning designs and designers, and the tools of the trade, from the Rotring pen to the Apple Macintosh and Adobe Creative Suite.

As the emphasis has moved away from the external commentator on design, it has instead become increasingly centered on the growing community of designers and educators who are motivated by the idea of what has been termed the "reflective practitioner"—the notion of designers commenting on their own practice. Designers are now regular contributors to journals and speakers at lectures and conferences. We have witnessed an avalanche of graphic design publications, all with varying degrees of insight, which focus on the processes and intentions at work. Educational programs and practitioners are beginning to build on this graphic design discourse and are, in the process, expanding the

definition of the practice. As a result, the epistemology of graphic design—its underlying methods and the critical study of its scope as an established body of knowledge— has expanded in turn.

Design and Education

The body of accepted knowledge that defines the discipline of graphic design includes its history and its practice, theories surrounding legibility, written language, and typography, a range of specifications and criteria relating to the printing profession, and codes and conventions associated with visual composition, color, and form, together with a range of theoretical models drawn from outside of the profession. Theories such as gestalt, for example, have been drawn from the discipline of psychology and employed by designers in their working methods and practices. These ideas have influenced the everyday discussion of graphic design practice and the language used by designers to explain their working methods.

This development is not without difficulties. Many institutions and commentators have struggled with terminology. Even the term *graphic design* is felt by some to be rather outmoded, embedded as it is within the traditions of print and static forms of communication, and alternative names, from visual communication to communication design—or rather nonsensical descriptions such as design for communication—have become more widely adopted in an attempt to appear up-to-date, modern, and in tune with the digital, interactive, individually focused, and personalized brave new world. The development of new technologies that (to an extent) empower and enable end users to shape, adapt, personalize, and contribute in their engagement with a

Research Methodologies

message or communication has led to something of a crisis of confidence within graphic design—at least within its academic, rather than much of its professional, context. Professionally, the core principles of the practice, tied to branding, advertising, editorial design, information design, wayshowing, packaging, and promotion, have remained fairly constant. The notion that new media would spell the death of the traditions and trade of graphic design is perhaps proving rather erroneous. Meanwhile, design education, which is forever trying to be on the cusp of new developments in order to prepare students for the future, may be in danger of losing sight of the value of traditional design thinking and methodology while chasing the next potential operating system or form of new media that will seize the public's imagination.

Although the range of changes in graphic design definitions and terminology at least reflect a positive desire to respond to social or technological change, the terms can become increasingly vague and meaningless. There is a danger of losing sight of the fundamental principles of graphic design as a methodology and an activity—a coming full circle to the view of the practice through its use of technology, as purely a formal, physical activity rather than an intellectual approach—a process of creative reasoning— employing logic, iteration, empirical and deductive reasoning, and decision making.

> . . . we see more and more attempts to rename graphic design: visual communication, branding, innovation, design research, service design, concept development, image building etc. etc. All these labels deny the material base of graphic design (printed matter) by cutting the ties that bind us to graphic production methods. These are deliberate attempts to let graphic design dissolve into visual culture without memory, without ideological weight, without material ground. Experimental Jetset, Iaspis Forum on Design and Critical Practice, 2009.

Equally, the line is blurred between graphic design and other forms of visual communication. That term is so broad and nonspecific that it might encompass film, photography, fine art, painting, sculpture, body language, dance, performance art, advertising, packaging, fashion, or architecture. This isn't to say that those subjects are not of potential interest or influence to the graphic designer, but to recognize that each mode of practice requires some degree of definition and specificity if it is to continue to grow and develop. A generalist approach is not necessarily needed in order to prepare design students for flexible roles and collaborative practice in the future. Teamwork requires that group members each bring specific skills to the shared table, and while a degree of openness to the exchange of ideas with others is obviously an advantage, a broad knowledge of visual communication without a measure of individual contribution and skill set is less valuable.

---

1. Hollis, R. (2001). *Graphic Design: A Concise History*. London: Thames & Hudson.
2. Frascara, J. (1997). *User-Centred Graphic Design: Mass Communication and Social Change*. CRC Press.

Problem/Idea

Generates

Solves

Research
Outcome

Research
Question

Finds

Defines

Research
Methodology

The Design Cycle

Design is an iterative process. Designers take a series of steps in the development of design solutions, incrementally moving forward in the pursuit of an effective final resolution. These steps may involve defining the problem more clearly, testing materials, color palettes, and visual composition, refining the quality and tone of the visual message, or critically reflecting on the range of prototype outcomes developed during the process. Although much design may be geared toward finding an optimum solution for a given problem, this process raises further questions and contexts through which to develop alternative and innovative outcomes. Happy accidents can lead to alternative resolutions or to new methods that could be employed by the designer on other projects, while failed experiments can help guide designers toward improved systems and methods, or can provide a critical base on which to demonstrate the effectiveness of the final outcome to the client.

A Manifesto for Higher Learning

1. No amount of ingenuity or creativity can create strong, clear, memorable design solutions from thought which is confused. This is why design is first and foremost a means of organizing ideas. Design is thinking made visible.

2. Opinion is welcomed but it is not enough. Your ideas must be substantiated through facts and testing, through research and evaluation. Build the confidence and the expertise to substitute "I think" for "I know".

3. Solutions will always vary according to context, interpretation, and vision. There are no absolute answers. Learn instead to ask the right questions and allow the nature of the journey to determine the best destination.

4. Regardless of any specific design interest or preference that you may have, in today's world all designers need to develop a multi-form understanding that is able to respond to multiple communication needs and platforms. Thus multimedia is not a component of contemporary design, it is its definition.

5. Beware of fashion—it encourages the idea that nothing is lasting and that you always have to be on the move. If you are never still you will never encounter profundity. Learn to stay in the same place and dig deeper.

6. Take nothing for granted. Learn to question what you think you know. Remember that the extraordinary is as likely to reside in the ground beneath our feet as in the stars above our heads. The capacity to create meaningful work is not simply measured by your willingness to explore new ideas and new territory but also through the ways that you are able to apply new ideas to old territory.

7. Design is a process of discovery through thinking and making, and our ability to discover is generally greater than our ability to invent. Think of your work process as a form of travel. Look for the things you don't know, the things that are revealed or inadvertently uncovered. It is easier to find a world than to make one.

8. We can make as a result of thinking and we can think as a result of making because thinking and making are not alternatives to each other. Both can be starting points as they are both ways of exploring ideas, testing methods, and generating knowledge. Both are forces of reciprocal power within the design process. One cannot take place without the other.

9. Every medium has its own voice, every form its own possibilities, every technique its own expressiveness, every visual language its own history and significance. These are your tools and every choice you make becomes a particular way of saying something. Learn your craft and make your choices knowingly.

10. Design does not exist solely in the realm of the intellect. The power to enlighten, to celebrate, to inform, and to disturb expectations also lies in the capacity to make emotional connections. Always use your head but never forget your heart.

11. The unique capacity of a designer is the ability to dismantle existing communication codes and to recombine some of their elements into structures which can be used to generate new narratives of the world. This tells us that method is at the heart of our practice and that design is not a piece of the puzzle, it is a way of putting the puzzle together.

12. You cannot succeed without commitment. You cannot thrive without passion. You cannot survive without pleasure. All these things, or their absence, will be reflected in your work. The resonance of design as a collective social project is in your hands.

Andrew Howard, "A Manifesto for Higher Learning," *Design Observer*, 2013.

Key Concept:
Critical Thinking and Critical Reflection

In concise terms, critical thinking in visual communication is an attitude and an approach to questioning the value of design proposals or outcomes that is grounded in theory and its relationship to making. It is more than a philosophical position: Informed or engaged practice is less about the ways in which theory can inform practice; it is graphic design engaged in the theory of practice, or praxis, with an equal emphasis given to both the theoretical and practical concerns of the brief. As the American designer and writer Andrew Blauvelt has observed, "graphic design does not begin nor end in the objects it makes."[3]

Critical thinking could be described as an important aspect of reflective practice—the consideration of the effects and consequences of graphic design activities. In general, reflective practice in graphic design could be described as locating the practice of graphic design as the subject of graphic design. Reflection in a designer's approach could encompass critical thinking about the meaning, function, and value of what is produced and its relationship to the intentions of individual designers and their audience.

Critical reflection is the process by which the designer reviews a project outcome or evaluates the success—or failure—of an experiment, by questioning its effectiveness against a predetermined set of criteria. These criteria may be either self-imposed or may be a part of the brief. Within an iterative design process, this means creating a prototype using one set of methods or tools, then stepping back from it and evaluating its success or failure to meet the requirements of the brief.

Criticality within our own personal practice can be seen in how we reflect upon our methods in order to locate our voice and articulate our position; criticality

within a community of practice or discipline can be about trying to challenge or change traditions or paradigms; and criticality can also be targeted towards other issues and ideas outside design altogether.
Ramia Mazé, *Critical of What?*, Iaspis Forum on Design and Critical Practice, 2009.

Within the commercial arena, market testing and measuring the effectiveness of a graphic message are often rigorously applied. Where the designer is working in a more speculative environment (for instance, within a project centered on pure research), the means by which effectiveness can be determined must be measured against the project's stated intentions. A project that sets out to make visible certain underlying characteristics of text within a book would need to be evaluated in ways that reflect and measure that specific objective. Readers could be asked to interpret the design in order to ascertain whether the implied meanings are made clear. The designer could also draw on contextual research that analyzes the range of graphic languages operating within the same arena, thus describing the range of already accepted codes on which to build.

---

3. Blauvelt, A. (1998). *Remaking Theory, Rethinking Practice; The Education of a Graphic Designer*. New York: Allworth Press.

Case Study 01
A Transferable Research Method
Designer: Matt Cooke

The drive toward a more social agenda for graphic design calls for a refocusing of the designer's role, indicating a need for a more considered discussion of the function and purpose of graphic design. Part of this discussion has been to explore how design might operate more effectively with a more methodological approach, which is achieved by exploring key aspects of the process of design thinking and making.

This project, by graphic designer Matt Cooke, originally published in the first edition of *Visual Research* in 2005, proposes that one possible answer to this question is to develop a design methodology specifically to help tackle such social problems. Although many designers believe that such a pragmatic approach would stifle creativity, Cooke set out to prove that creativity needn't be compromised and that the design process can actually be enhanced when working within a structured methodology. Cooke's project explores an unusual approach to the role of the designer in responding to a brief from a client. Rather than creating a series of visual proposals and variations of design solutions, he decided to concentrate on developing a working methodology for his client that could also be utilized in the development of future projects and provide a handbook for effective visual communication.

While working as a designer for a major UK-based cancer awareness charity, Cooke observed the way in which a detailed analysis and review structure was maintained consistently in the construction and evaluation of the campaign literature content, but noted that this thorough approach was not necessarily followed through and applied to the design process or practical implementation. The charity produced large-volume print runs of detailed public information material for distribution through local doctors' surgeries, but very little attention was given to developing appropriate visual languages addressed to specific target audiences.

Taking the launch of a live information campaign that was aimed at raising awareness about the links between obesity and cancer in young women as his case study, Cooke developed a working methodology that proposed, documented, and followed a series of steps toward achieving an effective and practical solution. By adopting a range of working methods from marketing and advertising, for instance, Cooke was able to create a successful solution to the brief. The testing of a range of proposed visuals, gathering of audience feedback, and the use of focus groups and surveys, as well as more traditional graphic design methods, led to the development of a highly sensitive and appropriate working methodology, which could be applied to alternative problems within the same field.

Cooke's working methodology is outlined within a self-produced handbook, which is divided into four sections defining each stage of the process. This presents a rationale for a method of visual thinking based on a schematic diagram of the design process, together with a step-by-step, transferable system for the construction and testing of a range of public information products. The handbook, which includes information on how to conduct market research and test the viability of alternative visual strategies, was given to the client in order to rationalize the system of new design commissions and to save on the duplication of work in the areas of research and development within subsequent briefs.

The first part of the process involved definition of the project, including aims and objectives, prospective audience, and potential visual outcomes. The step-by-

DEFINE DESIGN PROBLEM

IS THE PROBLEM SIGNIFICANT?
CAN VISUAL COMMUNICATIONS
CONTRIBUTE TO ITS REDUCTION?

NO

YES

DEFINE CAUSES OF PROBLEM

DEFINE TARGET AUDIENCE

BEGIN DIVERGENT SEARCH

VISUALLY RESEARCH TARGET

GATHER QUANTITATIVE DATA

GATHER QUALITATIVE DATA

ENHANCE DESIGN PROBLEM

AGREE DESIGN OBJECTIVES
Plan and implement ways to measure these

AGREE CHANNELS OF DISTRIBUTION

ARE CHANNELS AN AFFORDABLE
AND EFFECTIVE WAY TO REACH
THE TARGET AUDIENCE?

YES

DESIGN PROTOTYPE GRAPHICS

TEST ON MEMBERS OF TARGET

ARE GRAPHICS APPROPRIATE?

NO

YES

TEST IN SMALL SCALE ENVIRONMENT

RE-EVALUATE DESIGN OBJECTIVES?

NO

WAS THE TEST SUCCESSFUL?

YES

YES

ROLL OUT FULL SCALE

MEASURE EFFECTIVENESS

RECOMMEND IMPROVEMENTS

Stage 1
DEFINITION

Stage 2
DIVERGENCE

Stage 3
TRANSFORMATION

Stage 4
CONVERGENCE

Case Study 01
A Transferable Research Method
Designer: Matt Cooke

step process outlined by Cooke at the beginning of the project was broken down within each chapter of the handbook, and highlighted sections of the diagram indicate to the reader the stage reached in the overall process of the work. The use of strong background images by photographer Jim Naughten helps to give both a sense of visual drama and an overall cohesion to the series of project diagrams and illustrations.

The first section is entitled *Definition* and covers a range of activities that can help the designer define the problem to be solved. Through the analysis of the problem and the identification of a target audience, the designer can refine the brief and develop a clear set of objectives for the project. The second stage of the process, *Divergence*, covers a broad range of primary and secondary research methods, leading to a solid description of the context within which the work will function, alongside an audit of the range of related material that already occupies the same visual space. This part of the methodology also includes an analysis of appropriate visual languages relevant to the target audience. Further diagrams attempt to show the interrelationship between each stage in the process, demonstrating the ways in which each stage is interdependent, rather than a distinct and separate area of the investigation.

The third section, *Transformation*, describes the development and testing of a range of potential visual solutions. These experiments are tested by focus groups in order to generate feedback on a range of criteria: the use of color, choice of typeface and/or image, clarity, and legibility of information. At this stage of the project, Cooke attempts to build on the knowledge gained by conducting a thorough analysis of the context for the final work (stage two), allied to a strong understanding of

the intentions outlined in the brief (stage one), in order to propose well-grounded, functional visual solutions. By testing each of these elements separately, the designer hopes to gather more detailed and specific feedback in order to develop the structure of the campaign.

The fourth section, *Convergence*, details the production of the final design at full size, its implementation in the public arena, and the measurement of its effectiveness within this target environment. By incorporating specific design feedback within the data mapping and analysis of the campaign review structure, Cooke hoped to create a self-perpetuating system for gathering information and creating more effective solutions. This effectiveness can be measured in terms of both the quality and quantity of information delivered, against budgetary, production, and distribution considerations, and also in the responsiveness of the target audience. An overview diagram of the research and development processes shows a reflection on the procedures outlined in the initial proposal diagram, presenting the flow of the project as a more circuitous journey, rather than the linear route that was planned at the outset. This is an essential element of the critical reflection on the working methodology adopted during the course of the project.

Critical Reflections: — An Interview with the Designer
After graduating from the then London College of Printing with a Master's Degree in Typo/Graphic Design, Matt Cooke relocated to San Francisco, California, where he helped co-found Iron Creative, a digital agency with clients in the commercial, nonprofit, and arts sectors. As Head of User Experience at Iron, Cooke has led major interactive projects for Levi's, Dockers, The North Face, and Zipcar, to name just a few. He has served as an

INITIAL
FERTILISATION

EVALUATION +
REGENERATION

DEVELOPMENTAL
GROWTH

PRODUCTION

THE DESIGN
PROCESS

Case Study 01
A Transferable Research Method
Designer: Matt Cooke

American Institute of Graphic Arts (AIGA) San Francisco Board member; sits on the Board of Advisors for the Retail Design Institute (Northern California); and is a former adjunct professor at The Academy of Art University in San Francisco. He has lectured widely on design methods for social change, and his work has garnered numerous interactive and print design awards.

After undertaking this project, what was the professional feedback on the outcome? Was the guidebook implemented successfully?
The feedback was positive within the organization at the time. The team felt like this was an initiative we should use across the breadth of our education materials. Being able to quantify the performance of programs was felt to be of huge benefit. However, in those relatively early days of design thinking, it was always going to be hard to imagine the group continuing with the methodology after my departure—and indeed that proved to be the case, with those first projects acting as extremely beneficial case studies, rather than forming the foundation of an ongoing working model.

How has your subsequent career developed?
Process and developing a codified approach to design has formed a central tenet of my design practice to date. With the increasing influence of the digital revolution, and the complexity and scale of today's digital projects, a consistent yet malleable process is essential in providing the framework from within which to work.

How do you now feel about the methods developed within this project? Have you applied them or extended any further in your ideas and professional work?

I think the methods I developed and enhanced provided me with a really interesting tool and a more interesting mindset with which to approach the discipline of design. They have proven essential as I moved into the fields of User Experience (UX) and User Interface (UI) design—disciplines that embrace a more codified approach and rely on user-centered models to measure efficacy. As such I have merged my own theoretical discoveries with emerging interactive models to better serve end users and better frame the problem for my clients and design teams.

What other elements do you feel could or should be considered when undertaking a similar project—on critical reflection, how would you change or refine the process?
Today, design thinking has become common currency in the design field and beyond. Leading organizations value and covet the contribution design teams make and increasingly view design as central to their future success. If I could step back in time, I would more thoroughly embrace the design methods architecture that I put into place, taking the project even further and subsequently centering my entire practice around the proven value of a design thinking methodology. In today's climate, that is an easier proposition and position to take—in fact, now might be the perfect time to really capitalize on that strategy.

DEFINITION
A DEFINE DESIGN PROBLEM
A1 IS THE PROBLEM SIGNIFICANT?
    CAN VISUAL COMMUNICATIONS
    CONTRIBUTE TO ITS REDUCTION?
B DEFINE CAUSES OF PROBLEM
C DEFINE TARGET AUDIENCE

DIVERGENCE
A BEGIN DIVERGENT SEARCH
A1 GATHER QUANTITATIVE DATA
A2 GATHER QUALITATIVE DATA
A3 VISUALLY RESEARCH TARGET
B ENHANCE DESIGN PROBLEM
C AGREE DESIGN OBJECTIVES
D AGREE CHANNELS OF DISTRIBUTION
E ARE CHANNELS AN EFFECTIVE WAY TO
   TO REACH THE TARGET?

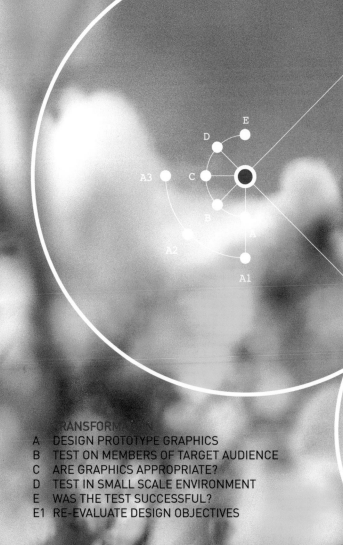

TRANSFORMATION
A DESIGN PROTOTYPE GRAPHICS
B TEST ON MEMBERS OF TARGET AUDIENCE
C ARE GRAPHICS APPROPRIATE?
D TEST IN SMALL SCALE ENVIRONMENT
E WAS THE TEST SUCCESSFUL?
E1 RE-EVALUATE DESIGN OBJECTIVES

CONVERGENCE
A ROLL OUT FULL SCALE
B MEASURE EFFECTIVENESS
C RECOMMEND IMPROVEMENTS

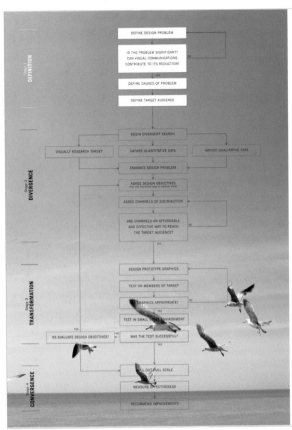

Stage 1
Definition

The first stage of the design process is called Definition. This is where the project is outlined in its initial form. At this stage the design team asks a series of questions to establish the nature of the problem and assess whether visual communications can make a significant contribution to its reduction.

The design team for this project included myself, Spencer Peppiatt (Design Assistant, WCRF), Maebh Jennings (Education Programmes Manager, WCRF) and Lisa Cooney (Education Assistant, WCRF). I should stress that I undertook all of the design work and only used the design team in this instance to approve ideas and develop concepts. The last two members of the design team (Maebh and Lisa) were also included because of their gender and age. WCRF clearly indicated at the start of the project that it was interested in communicating specifically with women between the ages of 16-34 (see page 28), and both of these women fall within this age bracket. Including members of the target audience in the design team gave us a greater chance of producing visual solutions that are effective in their intended environments. As Victor Papanek writes, "Most importantly, the people for whom the design team works must be represented on the design team itself. Without the help of end-users, no socially acceptable design can be done." (Papanek 1985: 304).

Define the Design Problem
The first objective of the design methodology is to identify and define the design problem at hand. This can be any issue that an organisation is attempting to tackle, from raising awareness of its mission to attempting to change behaviour in members of the public. Clearly defining the design problem at the outset gives the design team a starting point from which it can begin to tackle the rest of the project.

Members of the WCRF executive committee became aware that the obesity epidemic we are experiencing is strongly linked to an increased risk of cancer. Since this is a relatively new finding, WCRF wanted to raise awareness among the UK public that this association exists, and to create a climate in which maintaining a healthy body weight is considered essential. Therefore, the design problem was: to raise awareness that there is a link between overweight/obesity and cancer.

Stage 2
Divergence

The divergent search is where the majority of background research takes place. It is where the design team broadens the parameters of the design problem, giving itself the best chance of finding a suitable solution. At this stage the team should put aside any initial assumptions about the way the final project might look, and assess for the first time the project as a whole. This is a process of dismantling initial preconceptions. Jones refers to the divergent search as "...the act of extending the boundary of a design situation so as to have a large enough, and fruitful enough, search space in which to seek a solution." (Jones 1991: 64). The divergent search also provides an opportunity for the design team to reassess the original definitions of the project made in stage 1; to test their validity; and also to find out which of these established parameters are changeable and which are fixed. Jones continues: "In short it can be said that the aim of divergent search is to de-structure, or to destroy, the original brief while identifying those features of the design situation that will permit a valuable and feasible degree of change. To search divergently is also to provide, as cheaply and quickly as possible, sufficient new experience to coun-

teract any false assumptions that the design team members, and the sponsors, held at the start." (Jones 1991: 66).

The divergent search is also an attempt to get to know the target audience; to understand their likes and dislikes, to find out what motivates and stimulates them. In other words, its aim is to learn some of their values and attempt to learn their language – both verbal and visual. As Frascara notes: "In ethical communications, the producer has to speak a language that the audience can understand. If producers really want to communicate, that is, to be understood and not just listened to, they should remember that people can only understand things that relate to things that they already understand, and that it is impossible to communicate, therefore, without using the language of the audience in both style and content." (Frascara 1997: 17).

As part of the divergent search, the design team should pursue three main avenues of research: gathering quantitative data; gathering qualitative data; and visually researching the target audience.

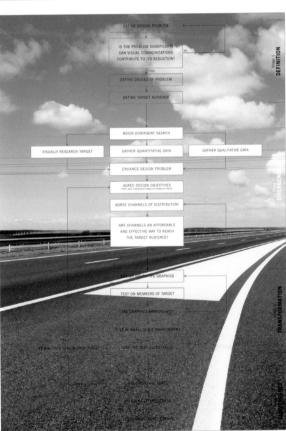

Stage 3
Transformation

Having conducted the divergent search, the design team has in its hands the raw material which, when filtered through its collective imagination, and honed by its design experience, evolves into a set of proposed visual solutions. At this point the design team draws on its understanding of the results of the divergent search and applies them to its knowledge of design. This is the process of Transformation and, as Jones states, "This is the stage of pattern-making, fun, high-level creativity, flashes of insight, changes of set, inspired guess work; everything that makes designing a delight." (Jones 1980: 66).

Nevertheless, this is not an innocent practice. The design team is trying to effect a change in human understanding. And the knowledge gained in the preceding stages gives them a greater chance of achieving this. It is essential that lessons have been learned by the design team and that they do not simply revert to personal styles, or comfort themselves by aping current trends. Frascara warns: "Frequently, designs fail because of the exploration and use of visual languages foreign to the audience. Others, imitating fashionable styles, tint messages with ideologies that could be at odds

with those pertaining to the intentions of their content." (Frascara 1997: 13).

So it is crucial, at the Transformation stage, for the design team to examine its motives behind any proposed visual solutions. Choices made because they appear 'cool' rather than appropriate, or 'trendy' rather than suitable, need to be rooted out in favour of ideas that might better serve the content and context of the communication. To some this may sound unnecessarily didactic, but to the user-centred practitioner, it is common sense. Frascara continues: "The excessive importance given to aesthetics has centred the attention of designers, design educators and design historians on the formal aspects of design, that is, on the relationships of the visual elements with one another. Graphic design is, however, first and foremost human communication, and what the graphic designer does is construct a pattern, something similar to a musical score, to organise an event that becomes enacted when a viewer confronts the designed product." (Frascara 1997: 14).

42 / 43

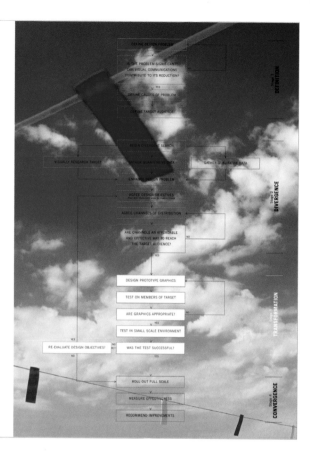

Stage 4
Convergence

This is the final stage in the design process. The background research has been conducted, design objectives have been agreed, channels of distribution assessed and prototype designs have been narrowed down. At this point the design team makes its final amendments and proceeds to roll out the product in the full scale environment.

Roll Out Full Scale
The ideal scenario allows the design team to do this with minimum effort, moving quickly from the prototype stage to completion. Jones emphasises the importance of moving swiftly to this point: "...to converge is to reduce a range of options to a single chosen design as quickly and cheaply as can be managed and without the need for unforeseen retreats." (Jones 1980: 67).

For the WCRF project, as discussed, it is not possible to roll out full scale until the tests have been completed in October 2003. However, this process was still

observed as the design team moved from presenting final prototype graphics to the WCRF obesity committee, to printing 20,000 copies of the leaflet for distribution via the organisation's Newsletter. Once the committee's comments had been implemented it was very easy for the design team to complete the leaflet's design. The committee, having been sufficiently reassured throughout the design process, was also certain that its ideas would be implemented appropriately and did not feel the need to see another draft of the design.

This unexpected benefit of the methodology – that is, instilling greater confidence in those commissioning the project – enabled the design team to complete the project very quickly and with a minimum of additional proofing.

52 / 53

CHAPTER 02
DESIGN LITERACY

RESEARCH THROUGH MAKING, ITERATIVE APPROACHES TO GRAPHIC DESIGN, PROBLEM FINDING, AND PROBLEM SOLVING

Visual Literacy in Design Practice

Design literacy, or visual literacy in design practice, is a fundamental concern for those involved in the creation of visual communication. The understanding of the interrelationship between formal considerations of shape, color, organization, and composition and the cultural signposts embedded in graphic communication is at the heart of successful and effective approaches to design. Although it is difficult to point directly to a considerable body of knowledge that might constitute an epistemology of graphic design, in particular theories and ideas that specifically relate to the act of designing, it is reasonable to accept that many of the formal aspects of design are informed by a wide range of underpinning ideas and theories.

Principles such as gestalt—meaning "unified whole" and drawn from psychology and the understanding of how human visual perception behaves—are at the heart of graphic design. Drawn from a branch of psychology that deals with the human mind and behavior in relation to perception, gestalt theory can be understood as being based on the whole being greater than the sum of the individual parts, and the implication of meaning communicated through the use of a part of an image or object, rather than the whole. Within graphic design, this theory can be applied to visual organization and composition based on the understanding that human beings tend to perceive groups or groupings in two ways: as being unified/similar or different/varied. The knowledge that elements on a page, for example, can be visually organized to direct the viewer or user toward certain readings or understandings is central to the activity of visual communication.

The ways in which visual elements that make up a design are able to communicate in a more or less effective fashion largely depend on a range of factors that are described by some of the defining principles of gestalt and perception. The fundamental principle or law of gestalt is known as Prägnanz. It is based on the human tendency to organize in a manner that is regular, symmetrical, and largely based on simplicity. The theory of the innate laws by which objects and their relationships can be perceived as organized or grouped is a useful building block for the designer in understanding how composition can communicate meaning to a viewer or user. This analysis of form and of relationships within a composition is informed by thinking about design in terms of concepts such as closure, similarity, proximity, symmetry, and continuity. These ideas, drawn from a branch of psychology that has its basis in the holistic, can be described in general as the whole being greater than the sum of its parts. In relation to the activity of graphic design, these theories relate directly to several design conventions that have become embedded over time simply as models of good practice.

Invisible Systems

Several other significant ideas can be drawn from outside of design and could also be considered as useful in describing the basis of a rigorous approach to visual/design literacy. These can be broken down into ideas concerned with composition, materials, color, and form.

The grid or system at work beneath a design—a structure created to ensure harmony and consistency within the layout of a book or poster—might be thought about using ideas related to the *golden ratio*, for instance. Also known as the golden section or the golden mean, this ratio can be found in nature, art, and architecture and can be described mathematically. Like symmetry—a concept that informed the work of many artists and designers in the past—it is argued that the golden mean is generally found to create a fundamental aesthetic preference in the majority of individuals. This theory informed the thinking of many Modernist designers in the early 20th century when they developed the principles of asymmetrical typography and composition. Like many of these rules or laws, the golden ratio's value is not in providing a strict code or doctrine of operation for designers, but rather in providing a rationale or explanation—a tool and a guide for understanding. The golden ratio has a strong relationship to the Fibonacci number sequence, which is a similar system, in this case based on number relationships in a linear sequence: each number being the sum of the previous two numbers—0, 1, 1, 2, 3, 5, 8, 13, 21, 34, 55, 89, and so on. This model can be applied to grid systems and even the relationship between type size and leading in text setting for editorial layouts.

Composition and editing can be considered using a technique known as the *rule of thirds*. This again has a strong relationship to the golden ratio and is based on dividing a given area into thirds both vertically and horizontally to create a grid structure of nine rectangles that have four intersections. This knowledge can be useful when constructing a layout and in the placement of type, images, or objects within a space.

Material Ideas

The understanding of the relationship between the materials employed in a design and the message that is given off is a significant factor that can be explained by the *theory of affordances*. This theory relates to the physical properties employed in a design—its materiality. For example, the format and cover of a book creates an effect or emotional response in the user whether through the choice of materials employed, the shape and scale of the book, or the use of illustration or photography. Although the photograph or reproduction does not afford anything, it triggers an association with the affordance of the object in the viewer's mind.

Visual Meaning

Other significant areas of design literacy involve the consideration of how color is used within an overall composition. The intelligent selection of color palettes and combinations of colors can be employed to create a design that is aesthetically pleasing to the viewer, but it can also work to emphasize hierarchies, structures, and relationships. These uses of color are directly related to formal composition within graphic design, but there is also a more complex consideration that requires another form of visual literacy on the part of the designer. This is in the area of cultural association and how messages are encoded and decoded by particular audiences dependent on issues such as background, education, and age, for example.

In many parts of the world, color is used to indicate meaning when associated with shape. Road traffic sign systems provide a good example of this. In the United Kingdom, a traffic sign that has a red border and a triangular shape is understood to mean a warning. Although there is some basis in our innate natural physical response to colors such as red—it raises blood pressure and respiration—our reactions to that color in that particular context are based on cultural preconceptions. Recognizing the triangular form of the road sign can be thought of as a learned behavior. It implies a reaction shaped through experience and

Principles of Gestalt

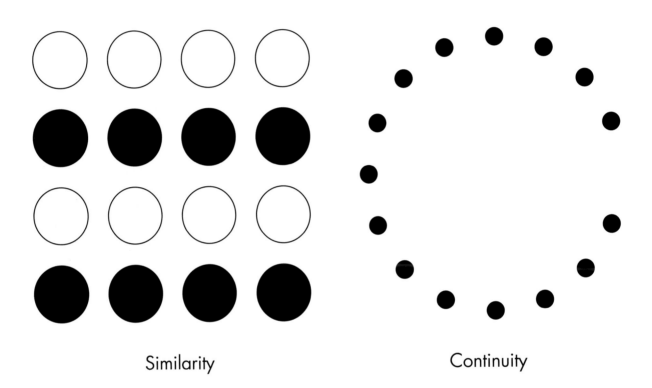

Similarity   Continuity

Similarity
This principle states that objects that share similar visual characteristics; shape, size, color and so on, create a connection in the viewer's mind implying that they are related or naturally belong together. In the previous diagram, horizontal lines of the same-sized shape appear to be grouped together because alternately they are either solids or outline.

Closure
In this example the effect is created in the mind of a white square floating above four solid circles, even though there is no square. The principle of closure states that when elements are aligned in such a way that we perceive that the information is connected, we tend to see complete figures even when some of the information is missing.

Continuity
The gestalt principle at work here is that closure occurs when an object is incomplete or a space is not entirely enclosed. Provided enough of the shape is indicated, we perceive the object as whole by filling in the information that is absent, thus completing the circle.

Proximity
Proximity occurs when objects or elements are placed close together. They tend to be perceived as a group or a unified whole. In the previous example, the vertical lines of dots that are closer together appear to be more related to each other or are understood as a single unit, separate from the single line of dots on the left.

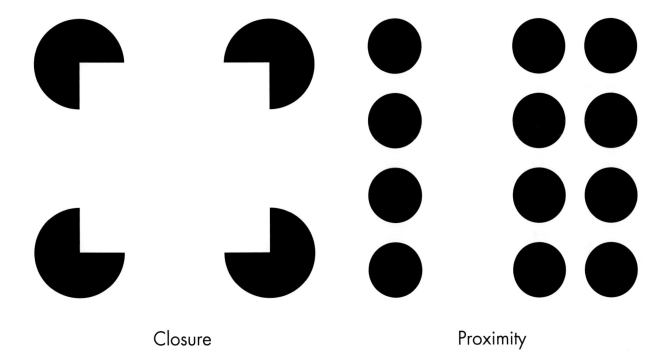

Closure   Proximity

Ways of Thinking

Max Wertheimer, one of the central and founding
figures of gestalt psychology, describes how thinking
can be considered in two ways: productive thinking and
reproductive thinking. The former is based on problem
solving and its relationship to the notion of insight: unplanned
and immediate responses to situations and environments.

The second mode, reproductive thinking, is based on what
has previously been learned and understood. These ideas
relate to a more considered approach to visual communication
and the processes at work in the creation of a design, and
to those factors at work in systems of communication—what
might be described as either immediate or intuitive reactions or
intellectual responses and readings.

Visual Literacy in Design Practice

social convention; it is agreed to represent a warning and is implicitly an instruction we are conditioned to observe and react to. In the United States, the convention for similar warning signs is based on an offset yellow square—the dynamic positioning of a simple shape again indicating a subtle sense of instability to the viewer.

This association has wider connotations for the designer who is required to create attractive and discriminable visual communication but who also, in order to be effective, is required to construct messages that can be widely understood. This depends on the individual designer's empathy and knowledge of the target audience. An awareness of how the individual components that constitute a designed message will be understood or specifically interpreted is a central concern to ensure that what is meant is what is communicated.

As technologies allow us to become increasingly interconnected, the manner in which we communicate has an increasingly global context. This places a further demand on the visual communicator to understand the significance of many of the smaller elements of a design. Shape and color, for example, and how they are understood, are not based on universal conventions and are open to interpretation. The study of the interpretation of meanings within symbols or visual constructions is known as *semiotics*, which also relates to areas such as image and text. Semiotics or semiology can be thought of as the science of signs and how they

operate in the world. It can also be understood in terms of connotation and denotation: the relationship between the literal or primary meaning of something and its secondary, interpreted meaning.

It would be easy to think of visual literacy in design as something that is only concerned with the formal aspects of composition, but for a design to work effectively, a wider set of cultural considerations has to be understood to ensure that the processes of interpretation and denotation are equally built into an overall approach to visual communication. These understandings provide the foundations from which effective design is created.

Complex social problems do not get solved by just doing things; things have to be done well. This requires effort, intelligence, cultural and ethical sensitivity, resources and institutional support. The design response to a social problem cannot be conceived as the production of a few posters and flyers that tell people what to do and what not to do.
Jorge Frascara, *User-Centred Graphic Design: Mass Communications and Social Change* (1997)

Reading a Text

The use of the word "text" refers to more than the printed word on a page in a book. It also encompasses other activities and items related to cultural production, such as the wide range of visual and aural forms of

---

Form
The shape or configuration of something, as against its location, context, or meaning. This could also indicate the pattern or structure of an object or image. In graphic design, this relates to the physical nature of the designed artifact, rather than the intention of the design or designer or any inherent message or communication.

Function
The performance or role played by an object or form. The service performed by a work of graphic design or visual communication. The classic phrase "form follows function" relates to the manner in which modernist architects and designers attempted to shape outcomes in relation to the problem being addressed, rather than taking a stylistically led approach to design.

communication. This would include, for example, a film, a wrestling match on television, or a building—anything that carries meaning and that could be read by an audience can be described as a text.

In the late 1960s and early 1970s, the French philosopher Roland Barthes began to challenge the existing idea that the author of a book could be considered as the central and controlling influence on the meaning of a text. In his essays *The Death of the Author* and *From Work to Text*, Barthes argues that while it is possible to trace the influence of the author in a text, the text itself remains open, encouraging the idea that the meaning is brought to an object—particularly a cultural object—by its intended audience. In this way, the meaning does not intrinsically reside in the object and cannot be reduced to an authorial intention. Barthes related "the death of the author" with "the birth of the reader," claiming that "a text's unity lies not in its origin but in its destination."

Many of these ideas helped to inform the wider theories associated with Postmodernism—a shift away from what were seen as dogmatic rules and regulations to a plurality of interpretations and an emphasis on the variety of readings and interpretations of a text. Such a critique was useful in developing our understanding of visual communication and graphic design, allowing designers and theorists to gain further insights into the way we create and read messages, but it was not without

difficulties as some measure of control over the myriad possibilities for interpretation presented proved necessary for any successful communication to take place.

Context
The circumstances that are relevant to an event or situation. In graphic design terms, this would indicate a clear description of the purpose or intention of a brief alongside secondary research into similar propositions or situations—historical or contemporary—together with audience expectations, the visual environment, and the background to the brief.

Concept
A hypothesis, theory, or idea. The fundamental aspects of the brief and the intention of the designer, usually in relation to a specified context, audience, and media. In formal terms, a concept also suggests a methodology or plan of action through which to test or pursue the idea.

Key Concept:
The Designer as Author

A significant shift in the range of approaches to contemporary graphic design has come about as a result of the debate surrounding the notion of *graphic authorship* and what this might constitute in the future for graphic designers. Although definitions of authorship in graphic design continue to be expanded and updated by designers, design writers, and educators, it is useful to consider a singular interpretation as a starting point for further debate.

Traditionally, graphic designers are involved in a process of facilitation: put concisely, the business of design is to communicate other people's messages to specified audiences—to respond to a brief that has been originated and defined by a client. This might be to provide general information (such as a train timetable or road sign) or to persuade a target audience about a particular product through its packaging and promotional design. This definition may be crude, but it is clearly applicable to the broad majority of design practices in the commercial arena. Graphic designers are commissioned to employ their skills as communicators in the service of a client.

The notion of authorship lies in the possibility that designers can also operate as mediators—that they can take responsibility for the content and context of a message, as well as the more traditional means of communication. The focus for the designer might be on the transmission of his or her ideas and messages, without the need for a client or commissioner, but still remaining fixed on the effectiveness of communicating with an audience. It might also arise from an exploration into an area of personal interest, or the observation of a real-world problem that the designer feels could be better addressed. The designer might establish an operational solution as a pitch to sell to potential sponsors or clients, in the same way that an inventor or product designer may create original products and models through which to present a business case to potential investors.

> *If we look at obvious online examples, increasingly the audience expects not only participation, they expect an active role in the creation … Forget "designer as author," you might now investigate the phenomenon of "everyone as author."*
> James Goggin, *Practise and Europa,* Iaspis Forum on Design and Critical Practice, 2009.

Graphic authorship can also operate in a commercial sense; a client might choose to employ a graphic designer because the designer has a particular visual style or method of working that would work in tandem with the client's message or product. This could be described as a designer's signature style. Many celebrated or well-known designers are commissioned purely because of a body of work that is concerned with particular themes or is popular with a particular audience. More recently, developments in new technologies and social media have resulted in a proliferation of participatory approaches to the construction of messages and meaning—from blogging to online forums and debates to chatrooms and individually tailored content provision.

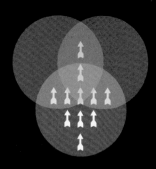

AUTHOR
DESIGNER
READER

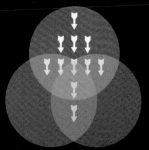

Case Study 02
Visual Grammar
Designers: Charlotte Knibbs,
Dan McCabe, Niall O'Shea,
Edouard Pecher

The following four case studies explore how individual designers have approached the area of visual grammar within their own personal projects. Charlotte Knibbs explores the form of the square in two and three dimensions. Her work plays with the movement of the square through planes and angles in two dimensions to create motion and tension through what might be termed optical illusion. This series of experiments is repeated in three dimensions using photography to recreate her earlier experiments, employing lighting, perspective, and angle or aspect of view to create optical effects and communicate with the viewer. Dan McCabe chose to take a similarly formal route in his interrogation of the geometry of the triangle, which then led to an exploration of the more complex star shape as both a formal construction and a cultural symbol. Niall O'Shea's work began with an investigation into the circle and dot and progressively grew to encompass an exploration of photo-mechanical reproduction and, in particular, the half-tone process. This exhaustive study involved a wide range of subtle and gradual changes in the scale and arrangement of key elements such as the dot and the line to create more or less detail in images and to generate patterns.

There is a strong link between these projects and the work of Edouard Pecher, which is concerned with visual grammar and generative systems and, in particular, the creation of a system of visual oppositions. These explorations are concerned with a detailed investigation of how form is related to key aspects of communication, such as meaning and perception. The ability to understand and control these key factors is essential in the design of effective visual communication. These projects are also linked by process and a focus on

the iterative nature of design research: the slow and methodical testing of an idea and the identification of potential opportunities arising from that research.

Charlotte Knibbs: Planar Square

Knibbs initially set out to explore the square, starting with some varied visual experiments to test everything she thought she knew about the form, its geometry, and its appearance. She began by altering the dimensions of the square as a simple four-sided figure, changed its angles and sides, and created an extensive visual audit of the changes she observed during the experiments.

When apparently warped and twisted, the shape of the square can be used to create many other varied shapes and optical illusions, in particular the impression of a two-dimensional form rotating and moving sequentially relative to an implied plane. Following these experiments in altering flat two-dimensional (2D) images of the square by skewing the original shape—creating rhombuses, parallelograms, and diamonds—Knibbs decided to extend the experiment into three-dimensional (3D) space, charting the changes to a fixed square through observation in perspective. She created a series of photographic exercises that attempted to mimic the same distorted shapes of her 2D geometric planes by varying the angle and distance of the lens (and hence the implied position of the viewer) to the square object mounted on a wall.

Following her experiments with 2D and 3D squares, Knibbs moved on to the 3D square form, the cube. Working with a group of fellow design students, she began to make simple investigations into the form of the cube and its relationship to light and perspective. They observed that shining a light at 90 degrees to the square would always form long, rectangular shadows

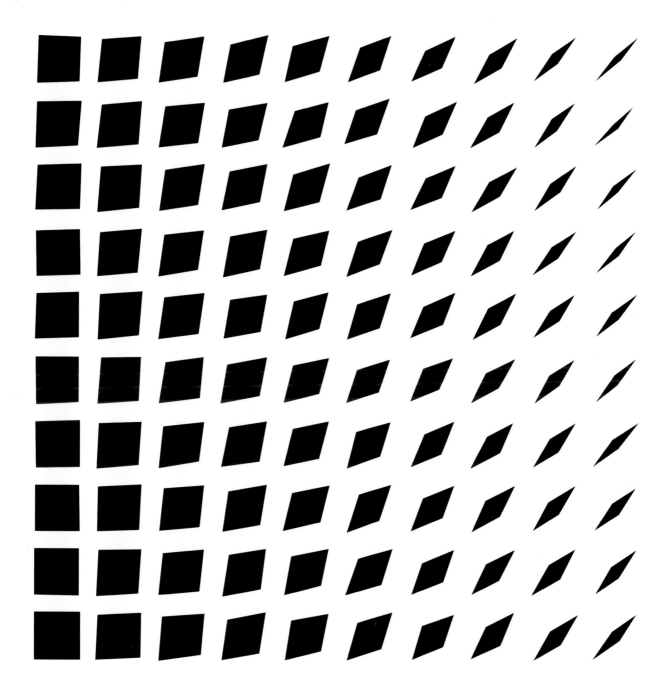

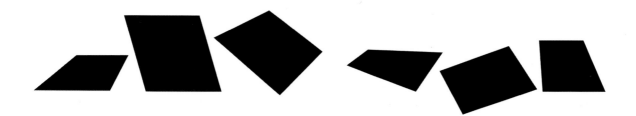

Case Study 02
Visual Grammar
Designers: Charlotte Knibbs,
Dan McCabe, Niall O'Shea,
Edouard Pecher

that stretched across the surface that the square was placed upon. Any changes to the angle of the light, the object, or the viewer, and the shape of the shadow created would completely change. These experiments are extremely simple, but each step informed Knibbs' further development on the project.

Dan McCabe: Star Shapes

Dan McCabe began his research through an exhaustive initial series of experiments exploring the geometry of the triangle, employing 2D and 3D techniques and primary and secondary research methods. Experiments included constructing hand-drawn triangles using a variety of tools, bending metal bars to create a range of triangular forms that could be played as percussion instruments, and investigating typographic form on a triangular grid.

He followed these experiments with an investigation into the contextual understanding of the shape through a series of questionnaires, asking respondents to draw a triangle together with further, more complex variations on the form. He observed that we are inclined to visualize a triangle in a geometrically balanced, upright form, despite the numerous ways it could be drawn. Perhaps the most intriguing results were to be found beneath the instruction "draw a star," whereby all but one respondent drew a form closely related to one of three simple variations.

This led McCabe to question why there were apparently clear commonalities with regard to how participants had chosen to visualize what is essentially a complex shape. He then chose to explore how many star forms he could geometrically generate from an equilateral triangle, through another series of geometric exercises. Having identified the star as a fascinating graphic shape, primarily constructed from triangles, McCabe began to

question what it represents as a sign or symbol within wider cultural contexts. His initial assumption based on prior research was that the star is incredibly rich in terms of its history as a religious symbol, and that there are many commonalities and contradictions in the comparison of its meaning across various cultural groups.

Niall O'Shea: Half-tone

The term *half-tone* is used to describe a reprographic printing technique that commonly produces a simulation of continuous-tone imagery through the use of dots or lines, varying either in size or in spacing. Although continuous-tone imagery might contain an infinite range of colors or greys, the half-tone process reduces visual reproductions to a binary image that is printed with only one color of ink in terms of black-and-white imagery, or four process colors for full-color visualization. This binary reproduction relies on a basic optical illusion—the fact that these tiny variations in tone are blended into smooth gradients and colors by the human eye.

O'Shea initially set out to explore the basic form and context of the circle, before moving on to the concept of the dot, and ultimately the visual patterns created in the production of half-tone images. Part of his working process involved the exhaustive documentation of a range of half-tone patterns and screens that were designed for image reproduction at different levels of detail and resolution. These screens were traditionally used as film overlays on continuous-tone images (such as illustrations or high-resolution photographs) in the production of printing plates. Variations in pattern include both round and square dots and lines of different size and thickness. Digital print processes have been steadily

Case Study 02
Visual Grammar
Designers: Charlotte Knibbs,
Dan McCabe, Niall O'Shea,
Edouard Pecher

replacing photographic half-toning since the late 1970s. Initially, electronic dot generators were developed for the film recorder units linked to color drum scanners. More recently, direct-to-plate digital printing has utilized stochastic patterns based on more scattered and less regular dots and lines in order to produce an impression of higher resolution and more natural images. O'Shea continued to apply his half-tone pattern analysis to the variation of dot size and line thickness in the reproduction of a range of gradients and special effects and images. Variations in dot and line clearly demonstrate the ways in which more or less detail might be revealed.

Edouard Pecher: A System of Oppositions

In his initial research, Edouard Pecher explored the relationship between fundamental forms such as circles, squares, and triangles. In particular, his investigation builds on how these forms can work in opposition to each other to establish contrast and create meaning. Using basic elements such as the dot and the line, the project explores how to create direction, movement, tone, texture, and scale. The acceptance that the majority of visual communication is based on the basic building blocks of these visual forms and their relationship to each other is not a singular and formal way of thinking about design but is more based in the understanding of the connection between the visual and the conceptual. The visual elements employed are described by Pecher as a "kit of parts"—the elements of a personal visual language through which he can begin to construct meaning for the viewer. This process of building an idiosyncratic visual language became focused on the development of what Pecher titles "a system of oppositions."

This subsequently led to a branding project that builds on the earlier work and the notion of visual oppositions to create a generative system for the graphic identity of a theater in Belgium. Generativity in this context relies on an algorithm or formula created by Pecher to produce a large number of permutations and relationships between shapes and colors. These rules allow him to create an identity that is not fixed in the way a traditional logotype would behave, across a range of print and screen-based applications. The system relies on the rules created by Pecher to create an identity that defines itself. There is a fundamental relationship between the system and the theater: the theater is based in a city and country where two languages are spoken and is also based on two locations on a north/south axis to each other. To create the system, Pecher created defining rules based on contrasting elements of squares, triangles and circles, colors, and lines. These elements are organized within an overall square shape. By using this delineated palette, he is able to create a visual system of a vast range of combinations and permutations and also develop a homogeneous and visually consistent feel to the identity.

The final outcome of the project is not simply an endless number of variations controlled and created by the designer. Pecher chose instead to refocus on how the system could become the basis of the identity, and how he could communicate the design of the system to other designers, who could then apply the rules he had created for themselves when working on design material for the theater.

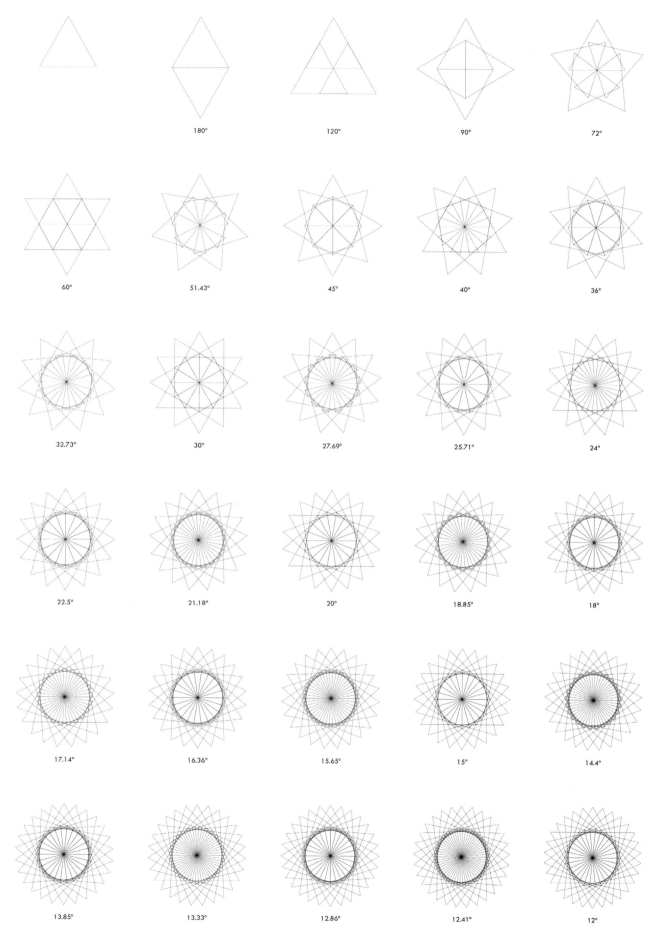

180°   120°   90°   72°

60°   51.43°   45°   40°   36°

32.73°   30°   27.69°   25.71°   24°

22.5°   21.18°   20°   18.85°   18°

17.14°   16.36°   15.65°   15°   14.4°

13.85°   13.33°   12.86°   12.41°   12°

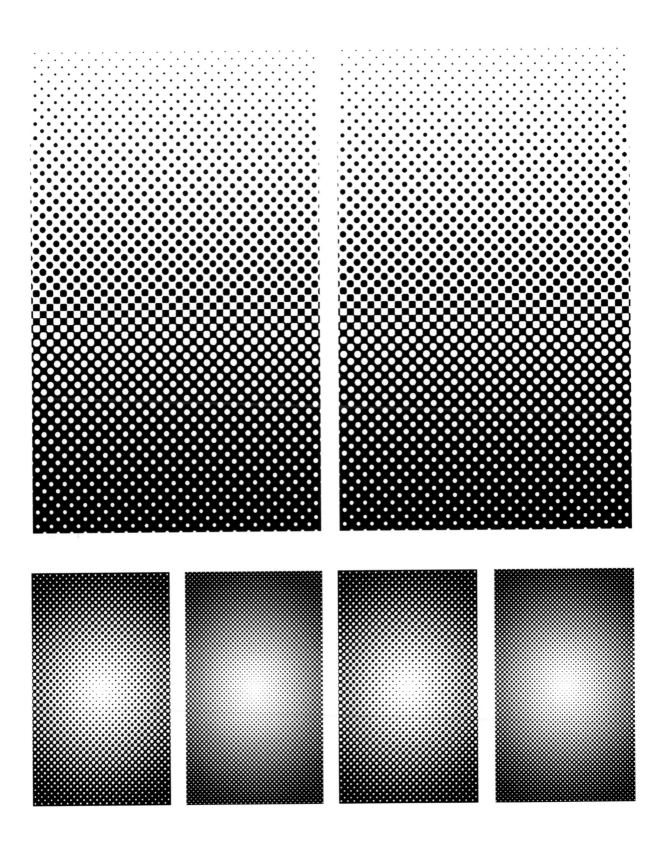

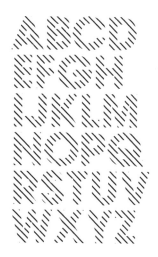

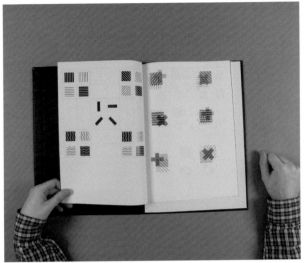

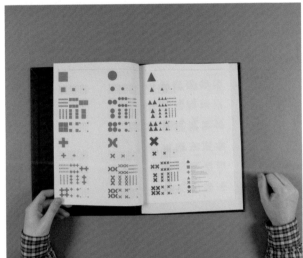

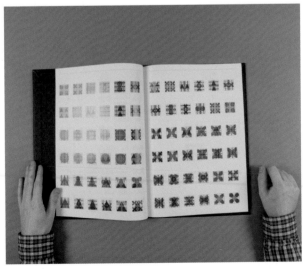

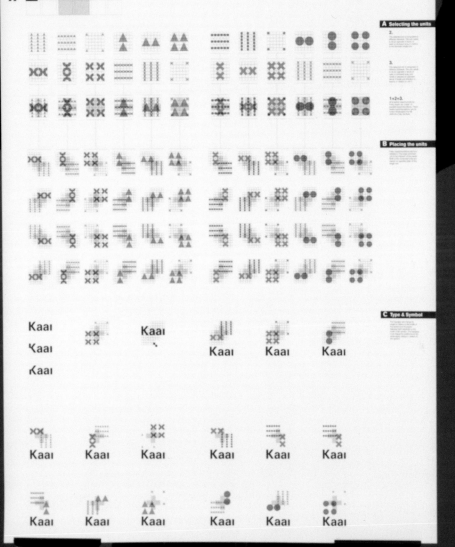

Design Activity 01: Design Literacy

Objective

The aim of these three related study projects is to allow you to investigate the principles of form and their function(s) in visual communication.

Within each project, an emphasis is placed on exploring core research methods. This is intended to help you to critically develop your approach to both practical and theoretical aspects of your work.

In the investigation of visual language, you will have the opportunity to reevaluate fundamental design principles and to consider their relationship to content and meaning.

The intention is to provide you with an opportunity to reassess your own approaches to practice in a process that might be described as delearning and relearning. Approach these exercises with an open mind, and try to avoid making assumptions or decisions based on what you already know from personal experience. The intention here is to embark on a journey of discovery, not simply to repeat accepted truths and meanings.

Part 1: Object

This brief asks you to explore the specific shape that you have chosen from three simple geometric forms (circle, square, or triangle), by producing a series of small-scale projects that investigate a range of specific attributes of visual form, including the following:

Space and form: *Line, plane, mass, void*
Time and meter: *Rhythm, order, motion, sequence*
Light and color: *Hue, tint, tone, saturation, transparency, opacity*

You should try to build a series of related practical experiments that demonstrate you have understood key factors in visual grammar such as: *mass, unity, fragmentation, meter, regularity, irregularity, motion, activity, passivity, space, order, randomness, sequence, continuity* and *interruption.*

Each of these themes should be investigated separately, and in turn, through a systematic and purposeful set of practical experiments. You should also explore the application of color to your formal investigations, testing, for example, the effects of *addition, subtraction, complement, contrast, tint, tone, hue,* and *saturation.*

Try to use methods that are not restricted to predictable outcomes by exploiting unfamiliar or untested media, locations, processes, materials, textures, formats, and so on.

Your investigations at all stages should be developed and documented with a view to producing a body of work that is based in analysis and developed in a systematic and organized fashion.

design activity 01

An important aspect of this part of the project and the next stage is that you concentrate on how you document each visual experiment or test and how these are presented. The focus on the process and methods you employ and how you will document them is a fundamental consideration of the project.

You must remember to focus on the nature and manner of your inquiry rather than the outcome. At this stage of the project, the journey is more significant than the destination. Although it is important as a designer to develop your approach to producing effective solutions or answers, this project is more concerned with the questions you ask and how you communicate them.

Part 2: Context
Brief 2 requires you to explore the cultural contexts surrounding the object you have been working with and to critically examine its uses in a representation, as a sign, symbol, icon, or metaphor. You should develop a series of related briefs, investigating a range of contexts, meanings, and values of the shape.

The questions you ask are up to you, but they might include the following:

• How have the meanings of the shape been constructed in social and cultural contexts—and why?

• What is the relevance of the shape to other fields, such as gestalt psychology, mathematics, or language?

• What is the relationship of the shape to historical, contemporary, linguistic, semiotic, philosophical, psychological, sociological, political, economic, technological, or other frameworks?

In generating design concepts, you should consider the following questions:

• How can you present a new and critical perspective to something very familiar and, in the process, challenge assumptions concerning it?

• How can you use it to generate insightful, novel, unpredictable, and communicable ideas?

• How can you develop a series of practical design methods that allow you to critically interrogate your object and to evaluate the resulting outcomes?

• Can you step outside of your own prior knowledge and worldview in the pursuit of neutral, logical design experiments that can reveal or question your own assumptions and prejudices?

Design Activity 01: Design Literacy

Part 3: Output

Brief 3 should be undertaken when the two previous stages have been completed. This brief requires you to revisit and critically reevaluate your earlier investigations with a view to focusing on a single, conceptual aspect of them.

You should develop this to a final, completed stage—a single piece of work (or a series of pieces) intended to communicate to a specified audience. Emphasis should be placed on generating a range of ideas and investigating possible ways to effectively communicate them. The intention is not merely to amplify earlier work but to use Briefs 1 and 2 as a starting point for generating a range of ideas that demonstrate you have now developed a critical, conceptual understanding of the shape.

Your final project might take the narrative form of a story, for example, and might be presented as an animation or as a traditional book employing words and images together. You might, however, elect to explore the shape you have been working with in a more applied manner, investigating the shape in relation to visual identity and branding, for example. The discoveries that you made in your investigations of form and context will have highlighted interesting avenues for further exploration and new insights that could be communicated to others.

It is important that you decide how you will work and in what context your work will be viewed. Remember, to be successful working in this way, it is important to establish the guidelines for how your project should be judged.

Working Process

You should begin both assignments by attempting to generate some ideas or propositions for your investigations. Try to put down on paper as many open-ended responses to the briefs as possible and as much of your existing knowledge as you can.

You should not look for final resolutions until the end stages of the project. Initially, you are asked to generate a series of visual responses and construct practical experiments that record your investigations. You are more

Essential Reading

Batchelor, D. (2000). *Chromophobia*. London: Reaktion Books.

Brewer, E. C. & Rockwood, C. (2009). *Brewer's Dictionary of Phrase & Fable*. 18th edition. Edinburgh, Scotland: Chambers Harrap Publishers.

Dondis, D. A. (1973). *A Primer of Visual Literacy*. Cambridge, MA: MIT Press.

Evamy, M. (2003). *World without Words*. London: Laurence King Publishing.

Gage, J. (1995). *Colour and Culture: Practice and Meaning from Antiquity to Abstraction*. London: Thames and Hudson.

Gage, J. (2000). *Colour and Meaning: Art, Science and Symbolism*. London: Thames and Hudson.

Kepes, G. (1944). *Language of Vision*. Chicago: Paul Theobald.

Leborg, C. (2006). *Visual Grammar*. New York: Princeton Architectural Press.

Lupton, E. (1991). *The ABC's of Bauhaus: The Bauhaus and Design Theory*. New York: Herb Lubalin Center of Design and Typography, Cooper Union School of Art.

Lupton, E. & Phillips, J. C. (2008). *Graphic Design: The New Basics*. New York: Princeton Architectural Press.

Müller-Brockmann, J. (1996). *Grid Systems in Graphic Design: A Visual Communication Manual for Graphic Designers*. Zurich, Switzerland: Verlag Niggli AG.

Roberts, L. & Thrift, J. (2002). *The Designer and The Grid*. Brighton, England: RotoVision.

likely to produce insightful, unpredictable, and purposeful work by seeking alternative iterations, developing and redeveloping both ideas and forms while maintaining a critical perspective.

You will also examine the object's functions and meanings by researching how they are constructed in diverse cultural contexts. You should use resources such as libraries, museums, and galleries and share what you discover with your colleagues. Do not rely on unsubstantiated Internet sources for your information.

Your practical experiments, contextual investigations, or other researches should be diverse but should also develop progressively as a series of alternative critical responses to the object provided. Each will benefit from a committed investment of time, energy, thought, craft, diligence, materials, attention to detail, and production values.

You can use any appropriate media you wish, and you should not hesitate to use methods with which you are unfamiliar.

Sketchbooks and Notebooks

Throughout the course of the project, you should initiate and progress your work by using a personal sketchbook, notebook, and/or research folder that will allow you to work through your conceptual processes.

Use your sketchbooks to generate ideas, to record textual, contextual, and visual researches (however messy), and to reflect on each stage of the project. They are perfect locations to test visual research methods: visualization, proposition, analysis, interpretation, and documentation.

Wilde, J. & R. (1991). *Visual Literacy: A Conceptual Approach to Solving Graphic Problems*. New York: Watson-Guptill.

Wong, W. (1993). *Principles of Form and Design*. New York: Wiley.

Further Reading

Crow, D. (2010). *Visible Signs: An Introduction to Semiotics in the Visual Arts*, 2nd edition. Worthing: AVA Publishing SA.

Heller, S. & Pomeroy, K. (1997). *Design Literacy: Understanding Graphic Design*. New York: Allworth Press.

Lupton, E. & Abbott Miller, J. (1996). *Design Writing Research: Writing on Graphic Design*. London: Phaidon.

Rudolph, A. (1954). *Art and Visual Perception: A Psychology of the Creative Eye*. Berkeley: University of California Press.

CHAPTER 03
ANALYSIS AND PROPOSITION
RECORDING, EVALUATING, AND DOCUMENTING A RANGE OF VISUAL AND VERBAL STRUCTURES, LANGUAGES, AND IDENTITIES

Research and Design

Research methods can be defined as ways of approaching design problems or investigating contexts within which to work. This chapter focuses on thematic approaches to problem solving and the construction of rational and logical systems of design thinking. By improving their knowledge of existing visual conventions, together with the development and application of a personal visual vocabulary, designers are able to make more effective use of their perceptions and discoveries, and to work practically and creatively with reference to a wider cultural context. Systematic research methods encourage designers to develop a personal and critical point of view through the recording, documenting, and evaluating of visual and verbal structures, languages, and identities in the wider environment, and then applying those findings within their own work.

A methodology is a body of methods (ways of proceeding or doing something, especially in a systematic or regular manner), which is employed in a particular activity such as the research aspects of a project. It is a logical, predefined, and systematic strategy by which to undertake and progress a project, to include methods of evaluation of experimental outcomes, a schedule for each stage of the project, and a stated intention or purpose in relation to a range of anticipated outcomes. It could also be employed to describe an approach to graphic design in general: a particular manner of working or a procedure used in the production of graphic design.

The adoption of a rigorous methodology that addresses the specific requirements of the brief and sets a series of boundaries within which to work on a broader investigation can help the designer to focus a project and define the exact problem, or series of problems, to address. Breaking the project down into a set of intentions, each with defined parameters and a predetermined level of background knowledge or experience on the part of the designer, makes the task more achievable and the goals of each stage of the process more explicit. Each of these areas is explained in detail within this chapter, showing the developmental process of a strategic design methodology relevant to the context of the brief. Examples of work illustrating key concepts from both the professional and academic fields are included to guide you through each stage of the process. These examples also help define each specific area of investigation explored and undertaken by the individual designer concerned.

Defining the Project
The first task for the designer is to identify what he or she is attempting to achieve with the project—a broad intention or set of intentions. Within commercial practice, this might be described in the brief as the message to be communicated, together with the target audience or market with which a commercial enterprise wishes to engage. In this instance, the work undertaken is a form of applied research. Alternatively, in an academic context, the aim might be broader: the proposal of a concept, or an idea for the student to visually investigate and respond to, in order to test a hypothesis, critically interrogate received knowledge, or gain further insight into a field of study. In this case, the work undertaken is a form of pure research. In either case, the terminology may vary, and the distinctions between different stages of the process may be more or less defined, but breaking down the proposal into separate areas of investigation and defining a project rationale is a useful preliminary exercise. Any design brief can be broken down into three areas for specific interrogation: (1) a field of study or context of the

project, (2) a project focus (often described as the research question), and (3) a research methodology.

Field of Study

The field of study (e.g., Where will the work be situated; What already exists in relation to the problem being investigated; and What function will the end result fulfill?) describes the context for the work. This could be the field of wayfinding and signage within information design or an audience-specific magazine page layout. First, the designer must research the field of study, to acquire knowledge of what already exists in that area, and the range of visual languages that can be directly associated with the specific target audience or market for the design. This would normally be done through a visual audit or survey of the proposed design context: What already exists within the field of study?

The designer needs to consider both the external position of the intended work (the explicit aim of the communication) and its internal position (the relationship between this particular piece of visual communication and others within the same context). This evaluation is very important, because contemporary cultures are saturated with advertising, information graphics, site-specific visual identities, and images related to entertainment or decoration. If a piece of graphic communication is to be displayed within this arena, the designer needs to be aware of how it relates to competing messages and how the problems of image saturation or information overload might be resolved in order to communicate effectively. The designer will become more familiar with a specific field of study through professional experience. By building a relationship with a particular client and their audience,

the designer can learn which forms of communication are likely to be more (or less) effective. Field of study research then becomes more intuitive, based on prior experience, accumulated knowledge, and learning, and then the designer can move more quickly toward an appropriate project focus and methodology.

Two contrasting approaches to design research are important to understand within this context: analysis and synthesis. Analysis includes the stages of a graphic design project that involve the collection and collation of data and the analysis or interrogation of existing properties and conventions therein. There are many ways to describe this aspect of a design project, dependent on the specific area of the design profession within which the work is being undertaken. For instance, within an academic environment, where a project might be described as occupying the arena of pure research, the analytical stage of the project might be described as the broad investigation of a field of study and the further specification of a project focus. In models of applied research, these terms could be supplanted with "problem" and "investigation" or "idea" and "experiment"; in each case, this stage of the project involves gathering background material and establishing the key themes and intentions of the brief.

Synthesis involves bringing together the range of themes explored in order to determine a way forward. Once a clear context and content of the design brief have been established, the designer is able to bring together secondary and contextual research findings with a range of experimental and practical methods of production in order to develop the final outcome or artifact. Again, these terms vary depending on the background of the project and the position of the designer, but synthesis in

Research and Design

each case implies the use of knowledge gained through research and the testing of alternative production methods in the planning and formation of creative and inventive design resolutions. Where the designer's approach has been informed through analytical methods, practical, creative development comes through the bringing together, or synthesis, of that acquired knowledge with practical iterations, experimenting and testing alternative methods, and strategies toward a proposed solution.

Design involves both analytical and propositional aspects of research. Designers need to be aware of the context within which their work will be read and the possibilities offered by audience familiarity, materials, and budget constraints. The solution also needs to be innovative, offering a new way of presenting the information. Different graphic design projects may involve each of these areas of research to a greater or lesser extent. The range and application of appropriate research methods depends on the brief or research question, the specific qualities of the message to be communicated, the project budget and timescale, and the relationship among client, designer, and audience.

Field of study or contextual research takes a variety of forms, dependent on the intention of the proposed work. Market research methods, such as intensive visual audits of existing material, might be appropriate to some briefs, whereby the designer seeks out other work in the same field and analyzes and compares the visual

forms of communication that are relevant and readable to a specific audience. This could mean a review of comparative products or visual systems, working with a client to establish their position in the marketplace or their aspirations to communicate with a particular audience. In most cases, sophisticated visual languages already exist that attempt to engage those audiences, and the designer should become familiar with their vocabulary, even if his or her intention is to create a new form of communication that sets itself in opposition to what already exists (i.e., what might be called an innovative or creative solution).

Cost implications are also important to consider at this stage of the project. The costs of materials, print reproduction, or other media (e.g., web design, digital storage, and so on), plus labor and overhead costs, all need to be taken into account against the intended budget for the project. The designer and client need to have a strong idea of the range of materials that are available—and, importantly, affordable—to them, and the implications of those decisions on the design. If the budget can only cover the cost of two-color printing, for instance, then those restrictions need to be put in place in advance and then turned to the designer's advantage in seeking innovative responses to the range of techniques and materials available.

The Project Focus

Once the designer has become familiar with the broader intentions of the brief, a specific project

Analytical
Adjective relating to analysis (n.)—the division of a physical or abstract whole into its constituent parts in order to examine their interrelationships.
The New Collins Dictionary and

Thesaurus (1992)
As a design method, this involves the designer becoming more familiar with the specific message or intention of the brief, the audience, appropriate visual language, and the client's requirements.

Propositional
Adjective relating to proposition (n.)—a proposal for consideration, plan, method, or suggestion.
The New Collins Dictionary and Thesaurus (1992)

This usually takes the form of a hypothesis or a qualified assumption, supported by some form of material evidence. Within graphic design, this means the definition and testing of a range of alternative potential solutions.

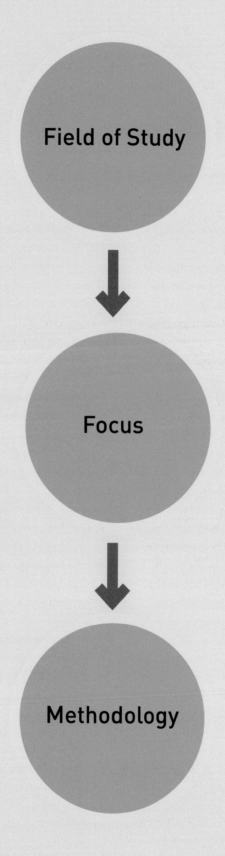

Research and Design

research question is needed to demarcate the exact intentions of the work to be undertaken. At this stage, the designer should be able to describe the message that is to be communicated to a specific audience, or within a specific context, and the aims and objectives of that communication. For instance, the goal might be to persuade the receivers of the message to act in a particular way (e.g., buy this product, go to this event, turn left at the next junction), to clearly communicate a particular emotion, or to identify with a subcultural group. The focus and specific research question may change during the lifespan of a project, becoming broader and then being redefined in an ongoing process of critical reflection and reappraisal. Narrowing down and refining a project focus might take place in several ways. Two useful models for the designer to use in order to ascertain the context of his or her work and define a particular research question are set out diagrammatically on page 65.

The first research model, which we will term the *context-definition model*, emphasizes the investigation of a field of study. In this model, the designer attempts to become more expert within the field of the brief through a thorough literature and practice review, and the resulting project focus is defined in response to an identifiable need within that area. The second model, termed the *context-experiment model*, still requires the designer to undertake a broad preliminary analysis of the field of study, but the practical work on the brief begins earlier in the process. This is usually done through a series of tests or experiments, which can be evaluated within the field of study, leading to a redefinition of the research question dependent on the results gathered. It is important here for the designer to not lose sight

of the original project intentions and to work through experiments in a systematic way. The context-experiment model will inevitably lead to some failed experimental outcomes, because each small test is an attempt to gain feedback in the definition of the project focus.

A Research Methodology

Once the problem has been identified, the next step concerns the choice of appropriate research methods (How will the designer research and develop the project in response to the context and intention?). A research methodology is simply a set of self-imposed rules by which the designer will approach or engage with a project or brief. Once the intention of the work has been clearly stated, together with a detailed mapping of the field of study and the definition of a focus and research question, the designer needs to outline exactly how he or she intends to develop the project and test ideas in order to create an effective solution to the brief—a plan of action.

The intention here is to develop systematic ways of working that lead progressively to a more successful outcome, based on experiments and visual testing, materials investigation, and audience feedback. The goal is to produce a piece of graphic design that is effective, useful, or engaging. The adoption of a series of strong and appropriate research methods should help the designer to make work that can be justified in terms of the processes used and that can be predicted to get closer to this goal. It is also important to plan the work in advance, including a rough schedule identifying when the designer expects to undertake each stage of the process, and the proposed deadline for finishing the project. Whether within the areas of commercial graphic design or design study, deadlines are usually given as a part of

Context-Definition

Context-Experiment

Context: Field of Study

Context: Field of Study

Focus: Research Question

Focus: Research Question

Context-Definition

Initial work in this model usually involves a thorough analysis of a broad range of secondary research, mapping the territory to be investigated and determining the range of work that has already been done within the field. Once a solid understanding of the context has been reached, the focus and research question for the project can be determined and a working methodology can be defined.

Primary research is usually beneficial at this stage, in the form of direct surveys of target audiences and visual experimentation to test appropriate visual languages. The results of these preliminary visual and contextual experiments can then help to define the specific project intention, together with an appropriate methodology that allows the testing of a range of potential outcomes.

Context-Experiment

Initial work in this model usually involves looser mapping of the territory to be investigated, an analysis of the range of work that has already been done within the same context, and a specified intention for the work within any revised context.

The focus for the project needs to be determined earlier than in the context-definition model, particularly through the definition of what the designer, and the client where appropriate, wishes to achieve. Distinct visual experiments to test appropriate visual languages and strategies are then conducted in order to determine a range of potential solutions. It is important that an overarching strategy is employed by which to critically evaluate and reflect on the relationship between each individual experiment.

Research and Design

the brief. Even where this isn't the case (e.g., when a designer is conducting a personal visual investigation), it is still important to plan a time frame for the project.

Another key question to consider at this point is: How do we measure results or quantify our findings? In setting up a series of experiments, which might involve trial runs with alternative visual strategies in response to a defined problem, how does the designer gather feedback in order to evaluate which of the visual applications is more successful? There are several ways to respond to these questions. Market research, especially in relation to product advertising and marketing, has developed some successful methods of testing materials and form through the use of focus groups, statistical analysis of surveys, and audience observation techniques. Some of these techniques can be linked to anthropology and the study of human interaction within social groups, whereas others derive from more scientific methods of data gathering and quantitative analysis.

It is also important to understand the differences between quantitative and qualitative methods. The designer will often use both forms of analysis, and their application may prove more or less useful depending on the brief and target audience, but the methods are distinctly different. *Quantitative analysis* is based on mathematical principles, in particular statistical methods of surveying and interrogating data. By producing several visual forms to test, the designer can place these objects in specific locations in order to count positive and negative responses from a target audience. This could mean conducting a survey using multiple-choice questions devised to score against a set of criteria. The data gathered could then be converted into numbers and analyzed statistically to find the most successful visual

form. As the size of the survey group or sample increases, we anticipate that the results will become more accurate.

Surveys can be a useful method for generating and gathering data in response to a proposition or research question—a hypothesis that the designer is seeking to evaluate, verify, prove, or disprove. However, a great deal of care needs to be taken by the author or designer with regard to the specific nature of questions asked within a survey and the range of anticipated interpretations and analyses of feedback received. The way that a survey is introduced to prospective respondents, the framework for the questions, the language used (which could imply the kind of response desired by the questioner), and even the tools and means of mark-making offered can all have a major effect on the kinds of responses received. If the survey questions are not strictly controlled or specific enough, there can also be a tendency for results to become blurred. Human responses to questions are not the same as results gathered within scientific experiments. Reactions to a visual message ("I quite like it" as against "I like it a lot") cannot be weighed in the same way as, for instance, the mass of a residue formed by the reaction between two chemical elements. People often have a tendency to score their reactions within the middle range of the options available to them, which can result in a statistical steering of data away from any radical or innovative propositions and toward a natural median or average. This can lead to an overemphasis on that data that is largely contained within a conservative, middle-ground set of replies, perhaps erroneously indicating a resistance to change.

Safety in Numbers
Qualitative analysis in design, on the other hand, is based on a range of subjective readings and responses by

Analysis

Synthesis

Field of Study	⟷	Focus	⟷	Methodology	⟷	Reflection
Claim	⟷	Evidence	⟷	Test	⟷	Exhibition
Craft	⟷	Tools	⟷	Process	⟷	Product
Intention	⟷	Theory	⟷	Context	⟷	Message
Question	⟷	Discourse	⟷	Audience	⟷	Thesis
Idea	⟷	Experiment	⟷	Production	⟷	Artifact
Problem	⟷	Investigation	⟷	Comparison	⟷	Solution

Research and Design

a viewer—though this may be the audience as receiver or the designer as originator of the message, depending on the stage at which the analysis is appropriate to the project—and is implicit in the surveys and focus groups mentioned earlier in this section. A key qualitative method for designers involves the analysis, or deconstruction, of designed artifacts. What this means in practice is reading explicit and implicit messages within a visual form, to determine the range of meanings that might be communicated to a prospective audience through the principles of connotation and denotation. If the principles of visual communication are broken down into the twin themes of the encoding and decoding of meaning (synonymous with the acts of writing and reading), then the range of implied messages and interpretations can be largely determined in advance. Graphic design usually operates within very specific boundaries, where the intention of the brief is made clear by the client or designer at the outset.

> *"Pure" information exists for the designer only in abstraction. As soon as he begins to give it concrete shape, to bring it within the range of experience, the process of rhetorical infiltration begins.*
> Gui Bonsiepe, "Visual/Verbal Rhetoric," *Ulm 14/15/16* (1965).

Certain vocabularies drawn from communication theories can help the designer to describe the range of activities involved in the process of visual communication. These methods are useful for the graphic designer, because they can help build constraints into the visual message in order to guide the viewer toward the desired reading, rather than a misinterpretation, of the message. By understanding

how the message might be received and understood by a range of different readers, the designer can try to avoid unintentional ambiguities and misreadings. These themes are explored in further detail in **Chapter 5: Theory in Practice** and **Chapter 6: Audience and Message**.

The establishment of graphic design as a subject and a discipline that has grown from its roots as a commercial activity to the current situation, where it is studied at graduate level and beyond, and is also the subject of research and numerous books, has been a rapid one, and it is worth reminding ourselves of the newness of the area. Depending on your definition of the discipline, it is only around 100 years old, and a good proportion of contemporary debate is largely still concerned with definitions, responsibilities, and purpose. This is especially significant when compared to the relatively longer history of related and tangential areas to graphic design from which ideas and descriptive languages are borrowed.

Claim ⟷ Evidence
Qualification

Claim and Evidence

Central to any design research activity is the relationship between the viability of the research question and the methodology employed in the exploration of the subject under examination. It is useful to consider this notion as if one was constructing an argument. The rhetorical aspect of graphic design is a central defining feature of the discipline. To create a successful argument, it is important to be explicit in two key factors: (1) the claim that is being made by the person putting forward the argument (the thesis), and (2) the evidence that he or she provides to support their claim (the qualification of the validity of the argument).

The assertion—the claim that the designer is making—should be both substantive and contestable. The contention proposed should be supported by relevant and valid evidence. This evidence should be introduced in stages; in some cases, it should be treated as if it were a subclaim and may need to be supported by further evidence.

The qualification of the design proposal—the evidence researched by the designer and put forward to support the claim—helps to fulfill several requirements in a successful design. It can help substantiate the choices made by the designer when presenting the work to the client, give greater credence to the visual vocabulary and methods adopted, and lead to a more thoroughly tested and therefore a potentially more successful outcome.

Key Concept: Denotation and Connotation

Simply put, denotation and connotation are terms used to describe what something *is* and what it *means*. Both of these definitions incorporate a range of variables and can offer up several questions. Objects may have multiple uses dependent on their context, and meanings are widely variable subject to who is interpreting them and where or when such interpretation takes place.

The term *denotation* is used to describe the primary, literal meaning of an image or a piece of communication, usually in relation to a particular target audience or group of readers. Like a name or noun, it describes what an object is, in and of itself, rather than what it means. This aspect of reading (decoding) and writing or making (encoding) meaning within a message is fundamental to all forms of communication. Denotation is central to encoding and decoding, because it is predicated on the first (most obvious or direct) interpretation of a symbol or sign, and therefore performs at the most basic level of communication without nuance or further implication.

Graphic designers need to be aware of the uses of particular visual signs and symbols, and their common meanings, within a target group. This is especially true within fields such as information design and the other areas of graphic design that attempt to reach a broad audience, and therefore rely heavily on the denotation of specific meanings within visual forms in order to make the intended message clear to as wide a range of users or receivers as possible. The context within which the message is to be read is crucial here, as are the specific material qualities of the visual form itself. For instance, it may be handwritten, typeset, drawn, photographed, printed, or on screen, each of which will affect the ways in which the message is interpreted.

Connotation refers to the range of secondary meanings, either intended or unintended, within a form of communication (such as a text; written, verbal, or visual). This includes the range of meanings and interpretations of an object or thing, its qualities, and impressions in the eyes of the reader. The meaning of the image and how we read it is not fixed by its creator or author but is equally determined by the reader. As such, a range of personal interpretations (and misinterpretations) of the meaning are inherent within a message across the audience spectrum. Such subjective understandings are in part determined by the receivers' worldviews—their education, location, culture, and experience that informs the way they see the world around them.

Anchorage and Relay

According to Barthes' theory of semiotics, there are two kinds of relationships between text and image: anchorage and relay. All images are *polysemic*; that is, they are open to endless different readings and interpretations, implying an uncertainty of meanings. Therefore, a linguistic message is often associated with a designed image, to guide its interpretation. In anchorage, the text anchors the meaning of the image by naming the intended denotation, helping identification. The text directs the reader through the signifieds of the image (and thus toward a meaning chosen in advance). In relay, the text and the image form a complementary relationship, and the text is intended to extend the initial reading of the image. Relay can often be found in comic strips and films. Peirce's theories of semiotics stated that three principal kinds of signs are used within visual, verbal, or other forms of communication: icon, index, and symbol.

house

home

Case Study 03
Non-Linear Design Research Methods
Designer: Lucy Brown

Educator and designer Lucy Brown chose to explore the design process itself, particularly in relation to design education and the exploration of appropriate research methods for students to learn and develop within their own practice. Brown's research question indicated her desire to encourage students to think laterally and to incorporate research methods beyond purely digital tools for searching and/or the creation of visual ideas. The research in this case centers on design pedagogy but also involves the use of design methods to evaluate and mediate potential innovative solutions to the teaching and learning of creative methods. The title of the final project, *Beyond Digital Technology: Introducing Undergraduate Graphic Design Students to the Non-Linear Landscape of the Creative Process*, positions the research within the context of a critical inquiry into the core principles and methods of graphic design education and practice, in a similar manner to Matt Cooke's reflection on design methodologies within the professional arena (**Case Study 01**).

From her professional experience as an educator, Brown observed that the advent of digital tools, and particularly the use of Internet search engines as an easily accessible route for gathering information on any particular topic that the designer wished to investigate, had had what she considered a negative impact on the design research process—as she puts it: (a) brief to (b) solution, via Google. She goes on to argue that:

> *Many entry-level students are blind to the "visible or distinctive" features of the non-linear creative process, and unaware of the options with regards to how and why they should traverse its landscape. They have grown up in an age of linear immediacy—of the digital Google map that tells them where to go.*

> *Choice is now linked to risk, and therefore causes anxiety. Notions of non-linear creative "travel," visual exploration, wandering and at times becoming lost seem irrelevant and frightening to many, meaning that the development of a non-linear creative process is culturally challenging.*

Brown undertook a series of exploratory exercises with her student group, leading them through workshops focusing on creative processes and methods—valuing play and conceptually open approaches to exploratory, rather than target-driven design research. One method, entitled *Evaluation of the City*, involved asking five people to consider their relationship with (a) the city and (b) the Internet as if it were a physical city, and to draw a physical map of each. The aim was to consider the similarities and differences between the participant's relationship with or experience of the city and the Internet, and to study the extent to which these relationships may or may not be considered as linear or nonlinear. These questions were also concerned with ideas surrounding psychogeography and the exploration or experience of both a physical and digital space.

She then set up the Landscape Research Group (LRG) as an independent network of design students and educators that would explore the value of creative workshops and open briefs. Successful applications deriving from this process would subsequently be implemented within the classroom in a more formal design education context, in what Brown terms a Non-Linear Workshop Series. Briefs were simple and deliberately limited in scope: (a) to present the concept of nonlinear visually, (b) to visually map the creative process, and (c) to explore a physical space in five

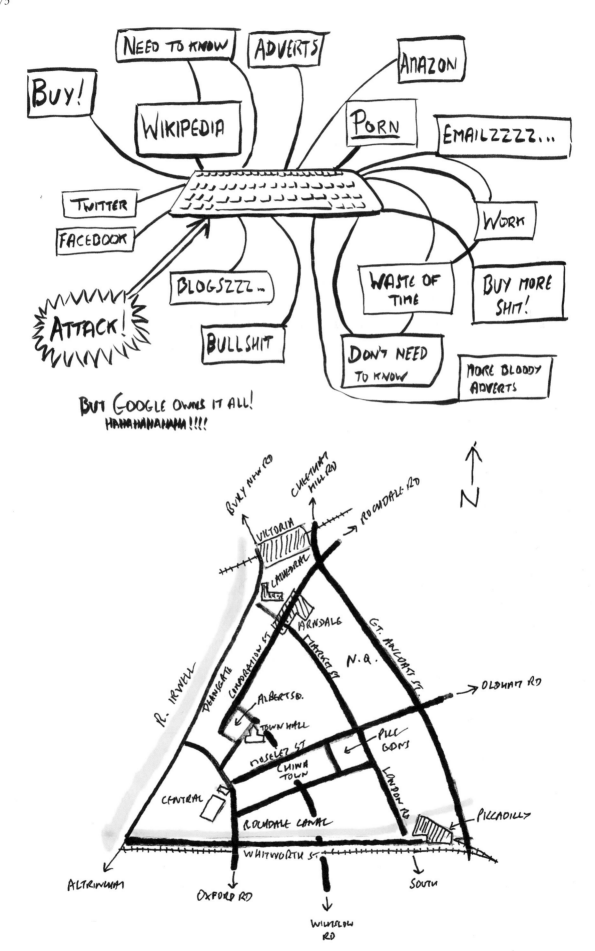

Case Study 03
Non-Linear Design Research Methods
Designer: Lucy Brown

different ways. The research exercises were intended to encourage students to consider the design methodology and to become more confident in the knowledge that the adoption of a rigorous process of investigation and discovery will lead toward potentially exciting and effective solutions.

As part of her initial research on the nature of student design thinking, Brown initiated a series of simple design research briefs with her case study LRG. The first asked participants to "source an image of the following 10 things: a sandwich, an animal, water, a fold, conversation, pattern, light, noise, speed, death," and Brown's stated aim was to "map sourced images on an axis of Google/Taken by Participant and Literal/Abstract in order to be able to observe patterns in behaviour." Of the 146 images submitted in response to the brief, 57 percent were sourced from Google and 43 percent were constructed by the designers.

The second brief asked participants to describe an initial reaction to the term *nonlinear*. This exercise was followed with a request to research the concept and to document the research process, then to create an image summarizing what nonlinear might look like. A further brief asked participants to explore the word *form* without using the Internet and to draw a map of their own creative process from brief to solution. The final design brief involved a more thorough process: participants were asked to go to a place that they would like to explore, and to choose five different creative ways to explore it. Responses involved drawing, writing, photography, illustration, collage, collected objects, recorded sound, mapping, and film.

The conclusions drawn from these exercises with a case study group informed Brown's next steps in

devising a series of workshops exploring creative practice that could lead to a teaching and learning curriculum enabling students to move beyond a reliance on digital search engines and toward more creative methods for visual research. The fifth and final workshop activity involves a field trip to an unfamiliar local landscape. A design brief is provided at the start of the field trip, asking the students to represent the landscape in five different visual ways. Students are asked to document the landscape as they walk their elected route in consideration of their five senses—sight, touch, smell, taste, and sound.

Feedback from student participants was positive, with many appreciating the creative possibilities opened up through unfamiliar research methods and the shift away from a kind of self-imposed pressure to arrive at practical solutions as quickly and directly as possible, rather than allowing themselves to become lost and to appreciate that experience as a valuable part of the process. Brown produced a handbook for the workshop series that could be adopted and adapted by other tutors and institutions in the creative field. As such, the project outcome is in many ways open-ended and speculative. Like Matt Cooke's design methodology that could be implemented by professional designers working in similar contexts, Brown's creative workshop series is designed to be taken up and delivered by other design educators as a framework for guidance, rather than a concrete designed outcome in itself.

Non-Linear Workshop Series

Your Name

PHIL PARKER

Draw a Line in the Box

Case Study 04
Modern Heraldry
Designer: Dan McCabe

Designer and educator Dan McCabe took a personal interest in the origins and practice of heraldry as a starting point for this practice-led research project. *The Observer's Book of Heraldry* describes heraldry as "a system of identifying individuals by means of hereditary devices placed upon a shield, which originated in Western Europe in medieval times." W. H. St. John Hope's book *Heraldry for Craftsmen and Designers* describes these "devices" as elements of "a symbolical and pictorial language." The elements (also called charges) that are placed on the shield are collectively referred to as being the coat of arms, and the shield itself is but one key component part of what is known as a full heraldic achievement.

The historic practice of designing and assigning heraldic achievements, or "granting arms" as it is officially known, is still very much alive. The College of Arms, which has existed in London since the 14th century, is legally responsible for recording and researching the genealogies of recipients who may be worthy of being granted arms. Far from being extinct, heraldry appears to have a ubiquitous existence within modern British society. It is a visual language that can be identified within a rich variety of guises and contexts; from fashion brands to council vans, castle walls to shopping malls, street signs to fine wines, football clubs to local pubs. Although looking distinctly armorial, many of these heraldic entities are far from being legal or authentic. In instances where such entities are not recognized, sanctioned, or granted by the College of Arms, heraldic experts would refer to them as being quasi-heraldic.

McCabe adopted a practice-led approach, conducting a series of individual but related experiments to explore the ways that heraldic language is constructed, used, and perceived. One experiment, entitled false arms, was motivated by the idea that original 13th-century heraldry was concerned with representing identity as opposed to what it later came to represent (and still does): genealogy and status. It explores whether it is possible to revisit those origins and generate arms that reflect 21st-century individuality through a limited choice of graphic marks and color. Questionnaires were given to a group of graphic designers, and arms were designed in response to the choices they made. The final set of shields were printed on a large sheet of fabric to mimic a traditional roll of arms. Other experiments visually surveyed and critically reviewed the existence and role of heraldic visual language within 21st-century British society. A typology identified and evaluated the most commonly found heraldic elements within these images: a crown, a shield, a lion, a helmet, and a banner. An analysis of these experiments highlighted that there are two distinct types of heraldry: authentic and bogus.

A Generation of Arms

McCabe's concluding investigation led to the final output for this research project. The purpose of this experiment was to find a way to use graphic design to engage the public in the subject of heraldry and challenge issues related to societal perceptions and misconceptions of quasi-heraldry. The initial phase of the practical research took place over two days at Southsea Castle, a small and well-preserved fortification situated in Portsmouth on the South Coast of England. With permission of the City Council, a point of contact was set up on the second floor of the castle keep. This consisted of a workstation, questionnaires, books, and various banners promoting the event. Visitors to the castle were encouraged to take part in the experiment by filling in a questionnaire. The

Case Study 04
Modern Heraldry
Designer: Dan McCabe

questionnaire was qualitatively structured to enable participants to provide enough details for a shield of arms to be designed and presented to them at a later date. The structure of the questionnaire was as follows: first, it asked participants to provide some basic personal details, such as their surname, age, sex, occupation, and contact email or postal address. It then asked participants to select the following elements: one of ten common shield divisions, one of five heraldic colors, and one of two armorial metals. The remaining questions then required participants to start to think more openly and to give both an animal and an object that they felt best represented their interests, personality, or profession. Finally, they were asked if they would prefer these chosen elements to appear once, twice, or three times on the shield.

One hundred visitors took part in the experiment, and their participation resulted in the generation of a unique shield of arms. Participants were made aware that even though the arms they had received were not legally proper in the eyes of heraldic authorities, they closely followed established rules of heraldic design. This is perhaps more than can be said for much of the ubiquitous modern quasi-heraldry that surrounds them. They were also informed about bucket-shop heraldry and why this practice is considered to be unethical. The resulting arms were presented within a large-format book, organized in alphabetical order of surname, and from youngest to oldest participant. The stylistic treatment of these arms is informed and influenced by three key factors: (1) following the strict rules of heraldic design; (2) taking inspiration from the Norwegian heraldic artist Hallvard Traetteberg, leading to a modern graphic style that can easily be digested and understood by a contemporary audience; and (3) resulting in an

intriguing mix of ancient heraldic symbolic conventions and modern popular cultural motifs. As in modern brand identity design, the use of such a simple graphic language can bring these elements together in a convincing way: logotype with lion, pictogram with panther. Each shield presented its own challenge with regard to ensuring that charges were perfectly visualized and that elements worked cohesively together to tell a story.

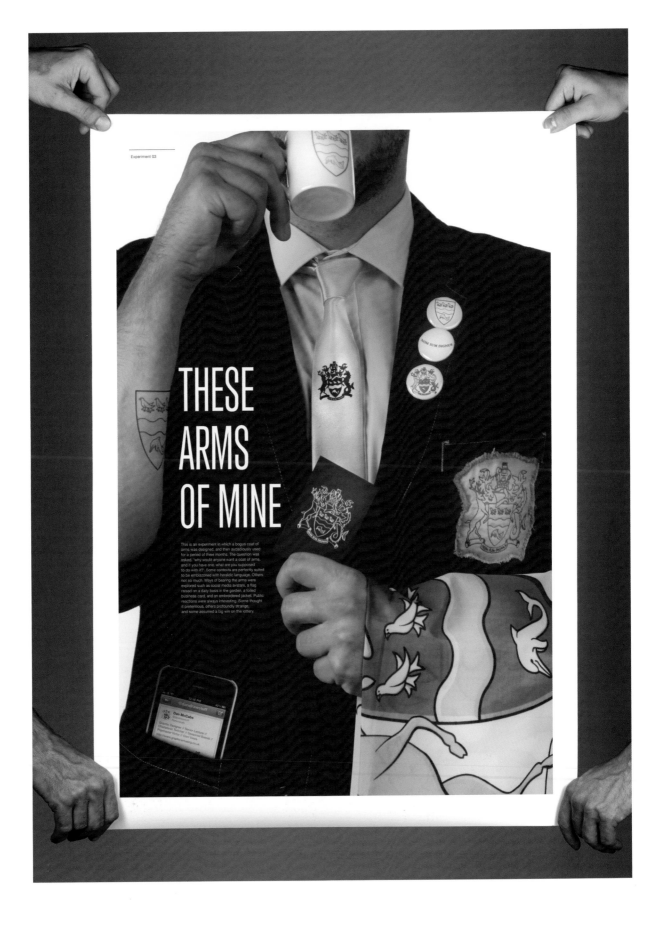

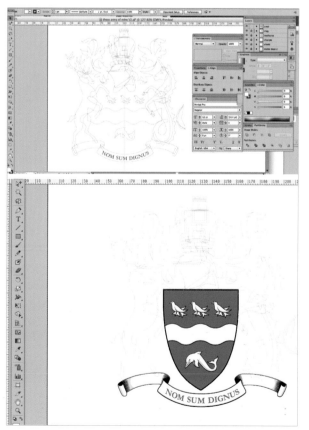

ABBOTT

LINCOLN-SINCLAIR

RILEY-NASH

BENJAMA

BENJAMA

BLAKEMAN

PERCY-LOOSEMORE

BOYNTON

BRODIE

MILTON

BURROWS

CARWITHEN

WILLOUGHBY

**Assumed arms
of Mr. Willoughby**

The Blazon
Azure between two candles argent
a laughing hyena's head affronty and
erased argent.

WRIGHT

**Assumed arms
of Mr. Wright**

The Blazon
Gules on a bend argent between
three spanners, two hanging
palewsie in sinister chief argent,
one fesswise in dexter base argent,
a rabbit courant warrenwise gules.

Design Activity 02: A Research Question

Objective

The aim of this project is to develop strategies for testing and adopting suitable methodologies in relation to your chosen subject area (field of study) and your personal set of intentions (your reasons for undertaking this project and what you hope to achieve by doing so), particularly in relation to the notion of independent and self-initiated project proposals. The outcome of this exercise will be a set of criteria that you will use to approach your subject and explore your research question in more depth as you move through the project.

The first part of the brief sets the scene for your project. You may have observed a situation that merits a design intervention in order to improve the experience of users in that space, or something that could be improved through the use of new technology. Equally, you may wish to simply find out more and become more expert about a particular topic. The motivation for this could be to demonstrate your design thinking and ability, to produce suitable work for a professional portfolio, or to further develop your own critical and practical skills in a particular area of graphic design.

Part 1: Establish Intentions
Create a presentation covering the following aspects of your project. The presentation should be designed to last 5 minutes maximum and can take any format that you prefer: a time-based digital presentation, a series of slides with a verbal presentation, or a written text. This should be supported by evidence of primary and secondary research, visual examples, and concise written and verbal statements.

Your presentation should cover five related areas:

1. Your <u>Field of Study</u> or <u>Context</u> (the subject of your enquiry)
2. Its relationship to <u>Graphic Design</u> as either <u>Subject</u> or <u>Method</u> (Is the core subject the practice of graphic design itself, or are you using graphic methods to interrogate or reflect upon another subject?)
3. The proposed <u>Audience</u> for the work (Who would be interested in your research? Who would benefit from a proposed design resolution?)
4. The <u>Intention</u> of the work in relation to its <u>Context</u> and <u>Audience</u> (What do you want the work to achieve and how would you like its audience or users to react?)
5. A number of potential <u>Research Questions</u> that you might employ in order to conduct your investigation

Part 2: Ask Questions
Work through your potential Research Questions one at a time, and critically evaluate their potential. Does the question offer the possibility of new discoveries or new ways of thinking about an existing subject? How does

the question relate to your personal intentions: Is the resulting work likely to lead toward the kind of outcome that you are seeking to create? (If you are looking to develop portfolio work, for instance, does the question allow you to create sophisticated potential solutions that will reveal your approach to design thinking and professional practice to a potential employer?)

• Choose one Research Question from this range of possibilities. Restate this Research Question in less than ten words. Design this statement as a simple A2 typographic poster.

• Using primary and secondary visual research, show the Context of your proposal as a visual construction, *without* the use of text. This must be output physically as an A2 print using whatever tools you feel appropriate (e.g., computer printout, photocopy, collage, illustration, screen-print, photograph, etc.).

Part 3: What Do You Know?
• Using visual methods and tools, communicate three things that everyone knows (or should know) about your subject.
• Using visual methods and tools, communicate three things that you have discovered about your subject that may surprise or confound expectations.

Part 4: Make a Visual Statement
Design an A2 poster that clearly summarizes and communicates your Research Question. This should be printed in a minimum of two colors and should be primarily visual, with minimal if any supporting text. You should be able to articulate the problem that you are investigating solely through visual communication, in the form of a collection of images, an illustrated composition, or a diagram, for instance. Bear in mind that you are visualizing the question or problem at this stage, not the resolution.

CHAPTER 04
VISUAL RESEARCH ANALYTICAL TOOLS

REVEALING SIMILARITIES, DIFFERENCES, PATTERNS, AND CONVENTIONS WITHIN COLLECTIONS OF VISUAL MATERIAL

Looking Closer

The relative newness of the profession, and the ongoing adoption of ideas and language from outside the graphic design discipline, have encouraged the idea that "design does not have a subject matter of its own—it exists in practice only in relation to the requirements of given projects,"[1] as the designer, educator, and writer Gunnar Swanson has written. Swanson also suggests that design is "integrative" and that the lack of specific subject matter belies its real potential to bridge and connect many disciplines. This offers both a positive and a negative interpretation of the strength and value of graphic design. The *content* of visual communication may be, by definition, extremely wide and varied, and as such, designers may regularly deal with a huge range of contexts, topics, subjects, messages, audiences, languages, and styles, but that should not allow us to become distracted by suggestions that graphic design therefore has no subject center or academic discipline of its own, or that it is purely a facilitator or mediator of external meaning, a conduit with little specific value beyond the careful arrangement of visual objects.

Several interrelated "loan ideas" from areas such as language and communication, for example, bring with them a form of words that allow the discussion of what Jorge Frascara has described as "visual communication design" in a manner that transcends the limited trade or technical language of the past and affords greater value to graphic design as a key subject in its own right. Care needs to be

taken, however, in utilizing such terms within a subject-specific graphic design context and avoiding in some cases the less helpful baggage of other intradisciplinary debates or contested definitions. In essence, what graphic designers and visual communicators understand by key concepts such as semiotics, deconstruction, or communication theory—related in large part to the context of their own practice—may differ from wider academic discourse that utilizes similar terms. This is actually common practice in other areas of study, and the increasing maturity of the subject of graphic design, as both an academic and a professional activity, should see these terms become more embedded and formalized within the discipline.

This chapter discusses the use of visual, design-led tools to aid discovery and to reveal similarities, differences, patterns, and conventions within large bodies of visual material. This includes an overview of the art of *looking* as a research method, visual matrices, typologies, the visual audit, the use of overlays, and what might be termed x-ray methods to reveal variations and changes in form and composition across sets of visual material. The use of meta-tagging in order to use interactive design methods for analysis and display is also touched upon, together with a range of print- and screen-based applications.

Visual Comparisons

One important area of design research involves the review, comparison, and analysis of existing visual

Semiotics
The study of signs and symbols, especially the relationship between written or spoken signs and their referents in the physical world or the world of ideas. Semiotic theory can be seen as a core strategic method by which graphic marks, texts, and images can be deconstructed and interpreted to determine their underlying meanings.

Semantics
The branch of linguistics that deals with the study of meaning. The study of the relationships between signs and symbols and the meaning that they represent.

material within the area that the designer is planning to produce new work. Within commercial design, that may be focused on a review of existing products, packaging, branding, and visual styling—often in conjunction with a business model analysis by a marketing department—to identify common trends, styles, and conventions. New design work will need to take account of such conventions, whether to maintain a sense of originality by avoiding common clichés or to fit within accepted norms in order for the potential audience to recognize its context and message. It's easiest to think about this concept in terms of products and major brands: the fact that a market-leading brand may use a particular color palette, type style, or logotype (e.g., Coca-Cola, Nike, or McDonald's) means that those specifications are usually heavily guarded, but it also presents a set of conventions that competing producers need to address. Many of those producers would use a contrasting color palette, in order to differentiate from their main competitor (e.g., Pepsi, Adidas, or Burger King), whereas others may seek to emulate the leading brand in order to communicate to prospective buyers by association. This latter approach is common among lower-value products, with some shifting further toward what might be termed a generic pastiche or imitation of the leading brand.

Decoding Design

Understanding the visual landscape that the designed message will seek to operate within is crucial for design research. Some aspects of that analysis involve an interpretation of prospective readings and meanings within comparative messages—that may involve the application of a range of theories relating to language, semiotics, communication, or audience (see **Chapter 5: Theory in**

Practice and **Chapter 6: Audience and Message**)—but it is important not to forget a close review of the formal, compositional, technical, material, and practical elements that are at work within those same messages. Primarily, this involves looking—*looking closely*—at the material. Such practical decoding and dismantling of visual material is perhaps avoided by designers and researchers at times, because it appears too obvious or too simple. We may think that it doesn't need to be said because it is clearly apparent just from looking at the material. Such suppositions can be flawed, however, and it can be easy to overlook the obvious. A formal review can help the designer to reveal common patterns and conventions or to refute commonly accepted clichés that may, in fact, be erroneous upon closer inspection.

A review of the use of color in the covers of a particular genre of books, for instance, might reveal expected findings (e.g., one could hypothesize that horror fiction uses a palette skewed toward darker tones and a preponderance of red, black, or blue, whereas romantic novels tend to use more pastel colors), but might also highlight the inaccuracy of such common stereotypes and could offer some surprises. Digital tools make it easy to reduce design compositions to simple color fields or to extract information relating to the underlying grid or typographic hierarchy. Such simple visual deconstructions can then be compared quantitatively, charting tonal palettes across a range of examples and drawing out commonalities and differences. Design relies on an acceptance and understanding of conventions (visual language) between originator and receiver, and a thorough formal analysis of common themes, styles, and patterns can be useful in interrogating and defining those customs and practices. It may also offer up some

Looking Closer

surprises, displaying design innovations and choices that step away from the norm and defy convention in order to offer a more original or creative model of communication.

The quality of visual objects might also be seen in terms of the craft skills employed by the designer in its realization, the time taken to produce the artifact (often evident on close inspection within the design's complexity, careful consideration of composition or media), and the nature of materials used. Such qualities and accepted conventions or principles become embedded in the visual language around us, allowing designers to tap into already existing styles, patterns, and visual languages, or to acknowledge and react against them.

We can learn a lot by looking. In the process of extracting information and searching for meaning we have the capacity to perceive and decipher all sorts of visual codes and clues. And we also discern time—an idea of how long something took to make. This too is information. It's a disclosure which could be described by saying that the work we look at emits its own "temporal signature." Whatever the case, whether we read in or the object reads out, we have the ability to gauge the investment of time encapsulated in the things we observe.
Andrew Howard, "The Aura of Time," *Design Observer*, December 9, 2014

Qualitative and Quantitative Analysis

The reading and interpretation of design artifacts normally utilizes both qualitative and quantitative methods. Qualitative analysis is normally based on subjective responses to visual forms and the reading of graphic material by a viewer. What does the visual message mean? What associations does the viewer have with the object? A form of qualitative analysis is often conducted by the designer him- or herself, in the form of critical self-reflection. The reading of images and visual signs through semiotic analysis is a qualitative act in itself: although the responses can be evaluated statistically or numerically as a form of quantitative analysis, the initial data gathered is based on human reaction to the visual forms and experiments presented, and is thus by definition personal and subjective.

Quantitative analysis is based on mathematical principles, in particular statistical methods of surveying and interrogating data (counting, in other words). By generating a batch production of visual forms to test, the designer can place these objects in specific locations in order to compare the range of positive and negative responses from a target audience. This could mean conducting a survey within the target audience group, perhaps with multiple-choice questions devised to score against a set of criteria. The data gathered can then be analyzed statistically to find the most successful visual form. Visual methods to analyze, compare, highlight,

Topography
A detailed description of spatial configuration. The word could be employed to describe a process of mapping, documenting, or recording, often with particular reference to what is occurring below the surface. Useful in graphic design research to describe an underlying approach to a project or a working method or process.

Typology
The study and interpretation of types (e.g., a person, thing, or event that serves as an illustration or is symbolic or characteristic of something). The phrase also relates to the organization of types and their classification for the purposes of analysis.

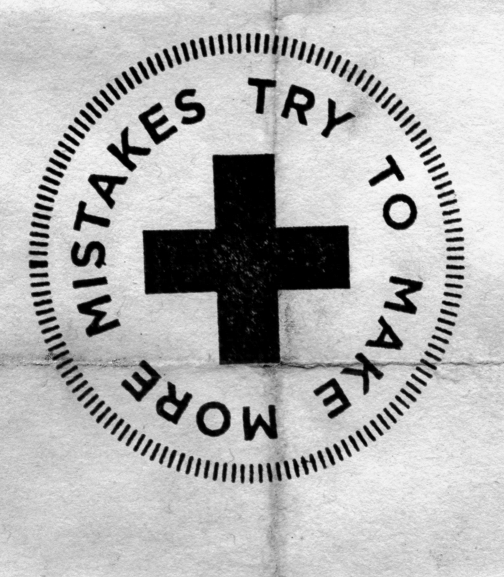

Looking Closer

and reveal patterns and commonalities can aid such a quantitative review. One simple visual device that can be utilized by the designer to reveal such information involves overlaying a range of examples of visual form as a kind of x-ray layered image in order to highlight similarities and differences. Examples can be seen in Orlagh O'Brien's work on pp. 100-107 and Paul McNeil's analysis of typographic glyphs and strokes on pp. 204-211.

New digital tools allow the designer to correlate and compare information more quickly and easily than before; image files can be tagged with meta-data and inserted into interactive charts or tables that allow comparisons to be made at the touch of a keyboard or the click of a mouse, rather than through hours of formal rearranging of physical material. The key thing to bear in mind here is the system that the designer chooses for categorizing the objects or artifacts in the first place—ascribing tags based on color, composition, iconic elements, type style, or other physical or conceptual properties of a range of graphic material—may or may not be useful. The designer/researcher should try to start out with a preselected range of possible common factors that could be argued to be important to the visual material under review—the use of color in political posters or photography in corporate brochures, or the frequent occurrence of particular typefaces or styles within a set of material, for instance. If some graphic elements or attributes appear arbitrary (or not specifically related to the core communication at work), then it may simply be the case that they are arbitrary and were chosen subjectively by the designer or client simply based on their own personal preference. Obviously, in these instances, the decoding of a range of material may not offer up any new knowledge or information.

Make More Mistakes

The iterative nature of the research process by definition will lead the designer along a range of variously successful, partially successful, or largely unsuccessful routes. In fact, if an experimental piece of visual communication is unsuccessful when tested with a target audience or in a specific context, then this should still be seen as a positive exercise in gathering information on the project focus and identifying directions with less potential for further development. By determining what does not work, as well as what potentially does, the designer is more informed and in a better position to arrive at a more successful resolution, as the classic quote by inventor Thomas Edison perfectly summarizes: "I have not failed. I've just found 10,000 ways that won't work."

Experimentation has become something of a buzzword in contemporary graphic design. Formally speaking, an experiment is a test or investigation, planned to provide evidence for or against a *hypothesis* (an assumption that is put forward in order to be verified or modified). When a designer is working toward producing a piece of work, a series of visual tests or design experiments might be useful in gathering feedback on potential new ideas and forms of communication—as part of the iterative and reflective process of design. However, experimentation is not a virtue in itself: it usually has to operate within a set of precise guidelines, delineating the intention and context of the experiment, together with the ways in which feedback will be gathered and analyzed, and how results will be measured. In short, a design hypothesis might presume that the creation of a particular visual form will communicate a particular message to a given audience. An experiment to test this hypothesis would then involve creating variations of that form and gathering feedback from target audiences or experts within that field of design in order to measure the relative success or failure of the work to communicate as intended.

This is not to exclude or diminish the value of *playing* with visual methods, materials, and form as an essential element of the design process. Sometimes the precise value and intention of a visual experiment may not be as calculated as that described previously. The exploration of potential tools for mark-making, or a playful, visually led creation of aesthetic possibilities, may at first appear illogical, random, and lacking a core set of intentions, but the critical reflection on such experimental investigations must still exercise some of the same criteria for formal evaluation regarding what has been discovered or achieved. The adoption or adaptation of tools, techniques, or modes of communication are useful experiments for the designer in and of themselves, even if their specific value at the time is not known. The Dutch graphic designer Karel Martens, for instance, is famed for his published sketchbooks and graphic notebooks, whereby early formal experiments with a typewriter or very simple contact print methods are reused within design concepts and briefs at a later date.[2] These visual notebooks can be seen as an example of the designer developing his or her own visual language and techniques, which can be drawn upon subsequently as the need arises.

Risk-taking, attempting radical new methods, and embracing alternative approaches are key to the production of original and exciting design. The phrase "make more mistakes," originally coined by Ian Noble as a principle design methodology, together with an encouragement for design students to extend their creative range, implies something of a conundrum. Normally, we are encouraged to avoid making mistakes, because they are by definition erroneous, valueless, or unhelpful, but in this instance there is a positive aspect to also consider. The making of mistakes demonstrates that risks have been taken, that the designer has thought *laterally*, outside of the box, and that the range of implied boundaries that delineate standard methods and practices have been bypassed in the pursuit of original and unexpected results. Innovative and new design *needs* to make such mistakes, rather than to rely on established conventions and ways of reflecting the world.

1. Swanson, G. "Graphic Design Education as a Liberal Art: Design and Knowledge in the University and the 'Real World,'" *Design Issues*, 1994.
2. Martens, K. (1996). *Printed Matter: Drukwerk*. London: Hyphen Press.

Key Concept: Rhetoric

Visual communication is closely related to the construction and presentation of persuasive arguments, because designed messages are intended to provoke a response or reaction in a reader or viewer. The concept of rhetoric is usually applied to literature and philosophy, and it refers to the strategic use of language as a foundation for reasoned argument. The classical art of rhetoric involves several distinct phases, which, in relation to visual communication design, may be described as (a) the discovery of ideas, (b) the arrangement of ideas, (c) the stylistic treatment of ideas, and (d) the manner in which the subject matter is presented. These correspond directly to graphic design methodologies such as concept, composition, style, and format.

Rhetoric traditionally comprises a range of figures of speech, including irony, antithesis, metonymy, synecdoche, pun, metaphor, personification, and hyperbole. It can be useful to compare some of these strategies with a range of similar methodologies used in visual communication, in order to differentiate approaches and to suggest alternative methods to explore.

The range of rhetorical terms utilized in graphic design might include:

Irony—a sign is employed to convey an oppositional meaning or to communicate a contradiction. Humor may often be used to imply an ironic, satirical, or contradictory position, with visual elements employed to highlight an underlying tension or incongruity that is often already familiar to the viewer.

Antithesis—contrasting terms are placed together in order to emphasize their differences. Graphic designers might use contrasting images or messages in order to produce a dramatic effect.

Metonymy—a word or phrase is substituted for another with which it is closely associated. An image or name could be replaced by a symbol that encompasses similar connotations, such as a crown representing a monarchy.

Pun—a play on words, quip, or witticism that exploits ambiguities in meaning for humorous effect. A designer may deliberately choose to employ an image or symbol encompassing more than one direct meaning or denotation as a simple, light-hearted visual pun.

Metaphor—a word or phrase is applied to an object or action that it does not denote, in order to imply a certain characteristic. Designers may deliberately use the range of connotations of a sign or symbol to reinforce a particular value.

Personification—attributing human features and characteristics to animals or inanimate objects.

Hyperbole—exaggeration for the purpose of emphasis or dramatic effect. This may apply to the relative scale of type and image, for instance.

Key Concept:
Parody and Pastiche

The notion of intertextuality—the ways in which an object or message relates to the language system that it operates within along with other existing objects and messages—is important to all forms of visual communication. A number of so-called rhetorical modes of graphic design (see page 096) relate to humor and the use of already recognized codes—cross-referencing other material that the reader is already aware of—in order to project a related message. In some instances, this is simply to situate the new message within an already understood context, but in others it can be to elicit humor or satire in respect to that context, to offer up a critique and questioning of accepted truths. It is worth analyzing these methods in detail and outlining the similarities and differences between each approach. Three key visual strategies can be described under the broad headings of parody, pastiche, and détournement.

Parody

The production of a new artifact or work created in order to mock, pass comment on, or make fun of an original work, its subject, author, style, or some other target, by means of humorous, satirical, or ironic imitation. Examples can be seen widely within areas of graphic design, particularly in such fields as activist and protest graphics (blending with satirical approaches in the latter), as well as the fields of advertising and entertainment.

Pastiche

The creation of an imitation or stylistic copy of an original earlier work, though with a different, underlying intention from a parody. In the case of parody, the work seeks to refer in itself to the audience's familiarity with the original and draws its impact through that recognition of context and connotation. A pastiche may imply a generally light-hearted stylistic imitation, which although humorous is usually respectful, but it may also be seen as a less valuable copy without any clear or intended reference to the original work.

Détournement

A term devised by the Situationist International, an art-based protest group active during the mid- to late-1960s in France and surrounding countries, *détournement* describes the turning around of power structures within images and other forms of mass communication, through appropriation and satirical intervention. The original intention of détournement was to break what the situationists saw as the Spectacle, the invisible codes and conventions of society and culture, which they believed supported and reinforced dominant ideological power structures and hegemonies. The strategy was later adopted by notable designers in the mid-1970s, such as Jamie Reid, whose record cover designs and posters for the punk group the Sex Pistols refined the approach within the context of abrasive, agitational, and politically confrontational graphic design. As a graphic language of protest and subversion, this style has continued to resonate to this day.

TERRIBLE'S TOWN CASINO

STARS & STRIPES
WIN YOUR SHARE OF $6,000!
WINNERS EVERY 30 MINUTES
FRIDAYS 5-9 PM

HONCHO'S BAR

BINGO BARN

BOUGAINVILLEA CAFE AND ROTISSERIE

RACE & SPORTS

TERRIBLE'S TOWN

Case Study 05
Emotionally Vague
Designer: Orlagh O'Brien

Some types of self-authored design work can be constructed in such a way that the design of the visual artifact is in itself a process of discovery. This project, by designer Orlagh O'Brien, sets out to gather feedback from a large range of respondents to a questionnaire asking how and where they experience emotions, representing patterns of commonly reported somatic and visceral experience, but firmly maintaining each person's idiosyncratic responses.

As a design project, the work sits firmly in the realm of pure research, with the design outcomes generated directly from the feedback gathered from participants in the survey, arranged and collated to reveal consistencies and shared or common responses. Although the data gathered could be seen as entirely subjective, by its very nature, and the visualization techniques as implying the application of qualitative methods, the range and sheer number of responses—there were 250 participants and a choice from 170 colors on the research palette—led to outcomes that can be read to an extent quantitatively as well as qualitatively. By employing a range of graphic design methods drawn from information design and typologies, together with creatively overlaying images to reveal patterns and commonalities, O'Brien was able to show how her respondents visualized their feelings through color, point, and line in relation to their own bodies.

Over time, careful refinement of the range and type of questions that were posed in the surveys allowed for more detailed and explicit responses from the participants. Although some control methods were set, such as the range of colors, the thickness of line-making tools, and the diagrammatic framework within which marks were to be made, the designer was careful not to direct respondents toward preset or existing conclusions. As a result, the methodology employed attempted to reveal common

patterns or tropes. In simple terms, the word *trope* refers to an object, image, or event that serves as a generic illustration of a common trend, which may be widely characteristic of a cultural group or society. Examples of tropes might include frequently occurring visual representations of common principles or messages within a group, dress codes, or styles and trends linked to a specific period or location.

Developing Research Techniques

O'Brien's initial research involved the development of a range of questionnaires, which asked participants to record visually where and how they felt particular emotions. Small test surveys were then conducted to evaluate results, refine the nature and phrasing of the questions, and adjust the means by which participants could make their marks. Initially, the survey also asked respondents to choose a pen from a limited range made available and to draw their own body, marking directly onto the image where and how they experienced particular emotions. O'Brien began developing methods to collate the information received and to overlay visual responses in order to reveal consistencies and patterns across the range of individual answers. However, interpretation of the responses by categorization or themes was problematic. The designer-as-researcher felt that she was imposing her own subjective analysis on the drawings. A better approach was to avoid this completely by changing the methodology—aggregating, rather than categorizing, the information gathered.

Refining the Data Set

As the survey was refined, it was redesigned to include a series of standard simple outline drawings of a human

ANGER

JOY

LOVE

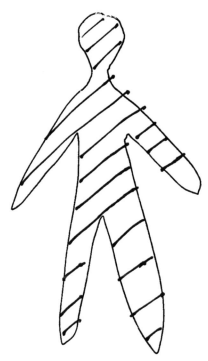

SADNESS.

Case Study 05
Emotionally Vague
Designer: Orlagh O'Brien

form, with headings detailing individual emotions such as joy, fear, sadness, and love. Once collated, the body outline could be removed if necessary, to reveal the patterns of emotion marks by themselves. Marks revealing the location of emotions and the area that each feeling might occupy were surprisingly consistent across several hundred respondents. A further question to show the direction of the emotions produced dramatic visual outcomes, which were overlaid by the designer to create aggregate visual maps of the collective results. Respondents to the questionnaire were asked to choose specific colors from a color chart that they associated with particular emotions, as well as describing where and how they felt those senses in relation to their own body. The results of these selections were then arranged by O'Brien in simple color bars to reveal similarities and differences.

Questions about the visceral emotion ranged from very open (qualitative or subjective judgments) to particular (such as asking respondents to indicate point and direction in relation to the drawn figures on the page):

• How do you feel these emotions in your body?
• Where do you feel the emotions most?
• Do your emotions have direction? Yes / No
  (If yes please use the red marker to draw arrows describing each emotion.)

As the process of data collection also recorded personal information regarding the participants, the visual information could also be sorted and arranged by age, gender, and nationality. Visual data was then collected, identifying the location on participants' bodies where they felt emotions and the color and direction that they associated with each feeling, in order to create a working

database of visual material. This method of working as part of a research project could also be described as analytical research, in that it examines a large body of qualitative data and allows a comparative analysis to be made between a large number of individual responses to the survey.

This visual material can be seen as a summary of the research process, with further testing and exploration detailed on the project website, and O'Brien's more recent *Pulse of the People Ireland* project at:
www.emotionallyvague.com
www.emotionallyvague.wordpress.com
http://pulseofthepeople.ie

Critical Reflections:—An Interview with the Designer
Orlagh O'Brien is an independent design consultant with more than thirteen years of experience in branding, corporate presentations, annual reports, and promotion for clients such as Vodafone, Safefood, Tourism Ireland, Diageo, Brown Thomas, Áras an Úachtaráin, Bulmers, and Toyota. She has worked for established agencies in Dublin, London, and Sydney (Designworks, Language, Maxwell Rogers, Heywood Innovation, and Landor) and was part of the team that won Ireland's top design award in 2002, the ICAD Gold Bell.

After undertaking this project, how was the outcome received, by academic and/or professional audiences?
A number of academic staff at the university were very interested in the project, and I was offered an opportunity to present the work to undergraduates, which subsequently led to a few years of associate teaching with a great team very much interested in visual research. Professionally, the graphic design world didn't appear that interested, as data visualization was only just taking off then, and even

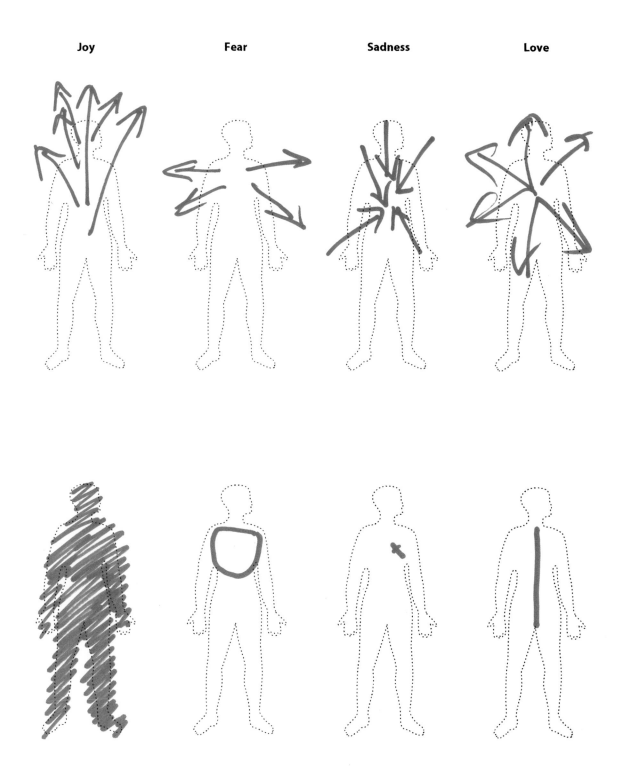

Joy   **Fear**   **Sadness**   **Love**

Case Study 05
Emotionally Vague
Designer: Orlagh O'Brien

within that area this project might be seen as a pretty arty experiment. I was insecure about my finishing skills: the traditional community of practice is attracted to the artifact—the polish of the final outcome or product, rather than the methodology or the journey made. Far more interesting responses have come from scientists in the United States and Europe, architecture researchers, user experience designers, psychologists, market researchers, innovators, and service designers.

How has your subsequent career developed?
Before the Master's course I worked in studios and large agencies without a sense of personal direction or a wider view of what design can be. Now I run an independent design practice here in Ireland, which includes art and social research collaborations. I enjoy the design process and working directly with clients and continue to apply a strategic and holistic approach to commercial projects. A couple of years ago, I collaborated with a social entrepreneur to do some research. The project *Pulse of the People Ireland* extended some of the methods from the *Emotionally Vague* work and expanded the questioning. It led to research work for a pilot scheme.

   Last year I went to Berlin to learn some digital art skills in order to move this methodology to a scalable level. So it's a work in progress at the moment. In terms of my commercial practice, this project is already almost ten years old, and it's persistently reminded me of how the boundaries around design don't really exist anymore. I'm moving into a more strategic space and am using drawing and observational skills more along the lines of service and experience design now.

How do you now feel about the methods developed within this project? Have you applied them or extended any further in your own personal practice or professional work?
The methods for this project came from what I had learnt on my Master's course, though the subject matter was totally different. So when the learning from one area was brought to a different domain, something interesting happened. I was lucky with the results, but in another way it was a natural step for me as I finally listened to my intuition. It's important to make space for analysis and method as well as listening to intuition and instinct. Both sides of the brain. In my practice, I'm aware of process: What is the content and data? How can we gather these? What is the intended purpose, and how can we design the process to achieve this aim? For me personally, the most powerful drivers are open questions. I use these in my personal spiritual life, my volunteering roles, and professionally with clients.

What other elements do you feel could be considered when undertaking a similar project—how would you change or refine the process?
At the time I didn't have access to the technology and analysis tools that are available today. It boils down to asking for help. The work forced me to ask for it, and it wasn't possible to do without the help of friends who carried out surveys by proxy, all the participants, and also a friend who created the database. In hindsight, I would have tried to define the help I needed even more, and maybe I would have got it!

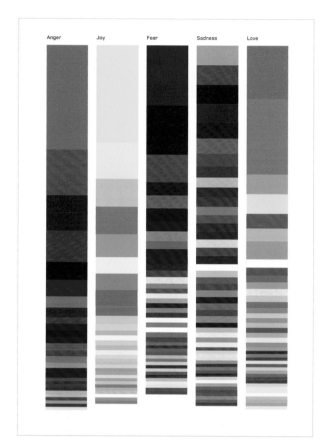

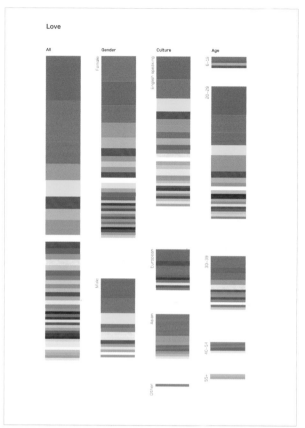

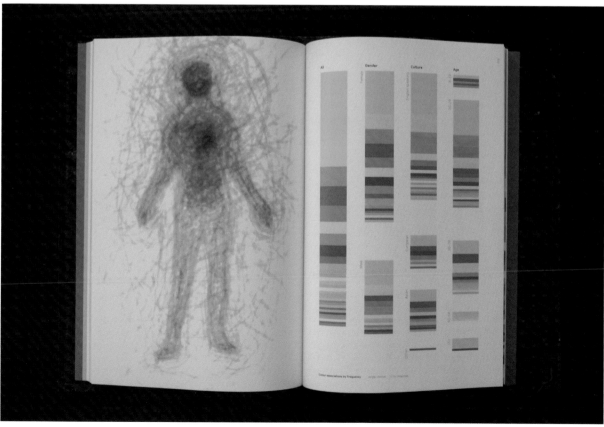

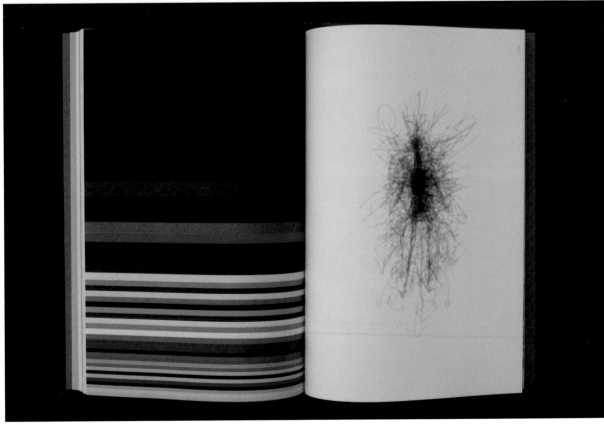

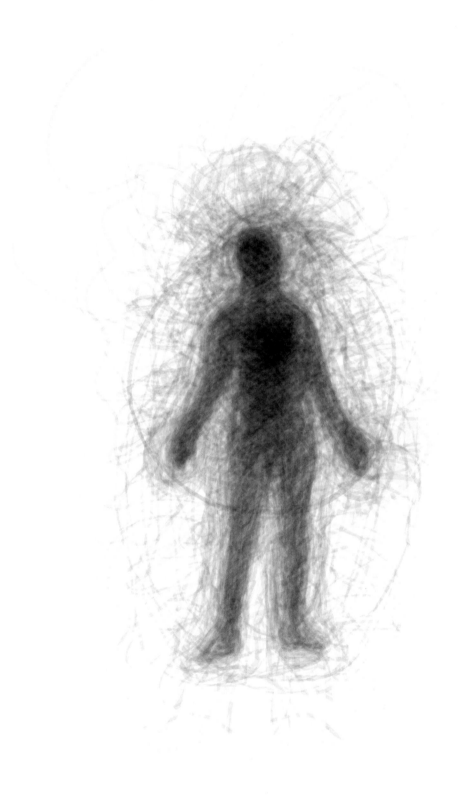

Design Activity 03: Design Analysis

Objective

The aim of this project is to develop your methods and visual thinking as tools of analysis. The outcome of this exercise is not necessarily an answer; instead, it demonstrates that a good research question enables a better understanding of what is being investigated and can lead to further questions and more focused routes of inquiry.

A typology is simply the study of types: a classification of similar things that have common characteristics or traits. The American architect and designer Richard Saul Wurman characterized the ways in which objects can be organized through what he calls LATCH theory: Location, Alphabet, Time, Category, and Hierarchy. LATCH can be a useful system of guidelines for arranging, grouping, and displaying visual material, and it can help the designer/researcher to discover or reveal trends, patterns, and idiosyncrasies.

In the context of graphic design and research, a typology can be understood as the creation of a system that allows a process of comparison to reveal patterns and connections that may not have been obvious to viewers when they first encountered the body of material being analyzed or organized. This project requires you to explore the use of the typological classification of objects in constructing meaning. It is designed to highlight the role of collecting, archiving, and taxonomy as fundamental features of research and analysis. The project provides the opportunity to gather data in a specific subject area chosen by you. It allows you to develop useful skills in documentation, comparative analysis, and inventive categorization and classification.

Designing a typology introduces you to a useful method for research that can be applied to other projects, either as a working method in itself or as a process through which to discover a critical position and research question in relation to the material under investigation.

Part 1: Gather Materials
You need to gather the materials for your collection. This will comprise a minimum of fifteen pieces, which can take any form. It may involve collecting physical objects or it could be a documentation of a particular

Key Texts

Bailey, K. D. (1994). *Typologies and Taxonomies*. Thousand Oaks, CA: Sage.

Dion, M. (1999). *Tate Thames Dig*. London: Tate Gallery.

Harvey, C. (1995). *Databases in Historical Research: Theory, Methods and Applications*. London: Palgrave Macmillan.

Klanten, R. (2008). *Data Flow: Visualising Information in Graphic Design*. Berlin: Die Gestalten Verlag.

Klanten, R. (2010). *Data Flow v.2: Visualising Information in Graphic Design*. Berlin: Die Gestalten Verlag.

Perec, G. (2008). *Species of Spaces and Other Pieces*. London: Penguin Classics.

Streijffert, C. (1998). *Carouschka's Tickets*. Stockholm: Testadora.

Tufte, E. (1997). *Visual and Statistical Thinking: Displays of Evidence for Decision Making*. New York: Graphics Press.

set of information using, for example, photography. Think laterally and creatively about what sort of content can be collected and arranged in specific sequences. You need to choose a theme or subject for your initial collection of things; it could be a set of small designed objects, packaging, book jackets, playing cards, record covers, logotypes, signs, or symbols, but there should be a rationale for your choice and some common connection among the different objects.

Part 2: Describe and Explore
You need to describe why you chose your particular subject area, as well as your initial observations and thoughts about the collection. You should then begin exploring the ordering of your body of material. Working at A3 size, using a photocopier or laser printer only, you must produce at least five variations, demonstrating at each stage a different approach to organizing your collection.

Take into account values such as scale, material, place of origin, function, and so on. Begin by implementing LATCH theory to your collection: how might the concept of Location or Time, for example, be applied to the material under review? Location might relate to place of manufacture or the specific site where the object was found or observed, whereas Time could describe a characteristic intrinsic to the object itself (e.g., date of manufacture) or perhaps a more personal relationship to when it was collected or the duration it has spent in your possession.

Part 3: Presentation
Begin to explore how best to present the organized material in visual form. This may not necessarily take the form of a series of photographic images but might be more abstract in its presentation: replacing numbers or values with colors or shapes, for example. Consider displaying the material in two or three dimensions—along a static timeline or sequentially within a simple frame-by-frame animation, layered on top of each other to reveal common formal elements, or deconstructed by form, composition, or color as a series of connected layers.

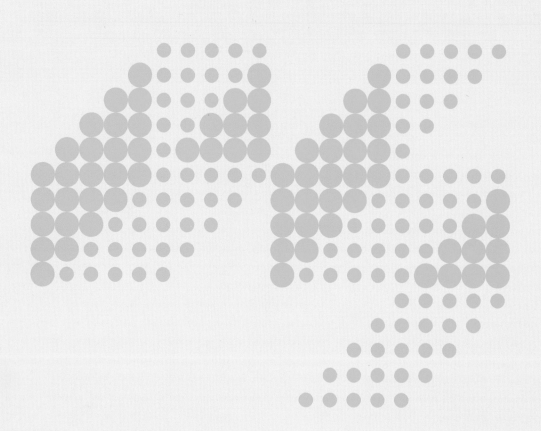

CHAPTER 05
THEORY IN PRACTICE
THE DECONSTRUCTION OF VISUAL WORK AND THE DEVELOPMENT OF NEW DESIGN STRATEGIES AND METHODS

Engaging with Visual Research

Visual research covers two main themes when related to what might be termed analytical and propositional methods—the deconstruction and interpretation of existing visual works and the development of new design strategies and methods. Many analytical models from across a range of art history and cultural theory focus on the former—the reading of images—but far fewer studies relate to the actual construction of graphic design messages.

In order to develop tools for the analysis of design objects and artifacts, it is necessary to become familiar with terminology borrowed from a range of disciplines outside of the traditional role of the graphic designer. Some of these terms might be introduced to design students as part of their wider cultural studies or visual culture and theory program, but they are often kept distinct from the range of practical activities that occur within the design studio.

It is important for designers to understand the vocabulary associated with the analysis of texts—by which we mean both visual and textual forms of communication—in order to reflect more clearly on the decisions made within their own work. As discussed in **Chapter 2**, it is useful for designers to break down this activity into a series of interrelated stages, mapping onto the basic principles of field of study or context, project focus, methodology, technology, and materials. The terminology used in the analysis of texts might be replicated in the description and construction of new material in order to qualify the designer's intention more clearly: this can be seen as the shift from analysis to proposition.

Intentionality is a useful term in graphic design in relation to the purpose or function of the designed object and the aims and objectives of its author or creator. It is often discussed in philosophical terms, especially in relation to language; some philosophers argue that

intentionality is characteristic of a concept or an intention. Within the field of philosophy, intentionality is related to mental states, such as remembering, believing, knowing, or experiencing, as well as to the concept of free will. In design research, a clear intention or set of intentions—such as "I want to learn more about this particular design method" or "I want to solve this problem in a creative and innovative way"—can help designers to focus their project and to define a specific research question.

Both qualitative and quantitative methods of design analysis might be necessary to conduct a thorough study of a piece of visual communication, either through decoding meanings in individual artifacts or through collecting and comparing a range of related examples in order to evaluate design vocabularies that are selected as appropriate to a particular context or audience. Visual research involves designers in a broad range of activities, which contribute to the development of new design propositions in several ways. First, designers need to understand the context within which the work is to be placed. This means that the range of materials already in existence, the expectations of the target audience, and the existing messages against which the work may be required to compete all need to be taken into account.

Traditionally, design education has worked with contextual visual research at the level of materials gathering and the construction of "mood boards"—rough layouts of a range of objects that relate to the message, giving an impression of the kind of feel intended by the designer at the outset of the project. Some of these objects and visual elements might relate directly to the envisaged resolution, whereas others are incorporated to denote emotional aspirations and the underlying feelings that the product is intended to evoke. Although this can be a useful exercise, particularly in relation to product design, advertising, and marketing, graphic designers also need to develop a more sophisticated and subject-specific methodology for analyzing a range of materials relevant to the proposed project.

The word "theory" comes from the Greek word theorema meaning to review or to reflect. The dictionary defines theory as an explanation or system of anything: an exposition of the abstract principles of either a science or an art. Theory is a speculation on something rather than a practice.
David Crow, *Visible Signs: An Introduction to Semiotics in the Visual Arts* (2010).

Familiarity Counts

It is important for the designer to understand the range of visual languages and texts that already exist in the space that the proposed design will occupy. All audiences have expectations with which they interrogate and interact with visual messages. The aim of innovative design is to relate to these already familiar forms (the viewer needs to be able to recognize the message being communicated) and to extend the visual language used in new and exciting ways (the design grabs the viewer's attention because it differs from an expected norm or convention). This means that the form of the visual language carries meaning, before we even start to analyze the content of the message itself. As Marshall McLuhan succinctly put it in his 1967 manifesto, "the medium is the message"; in other words, the ways in which we transmit and receive information have an important and direct effect on the content of that information and the ways in which that content is read and understood.

A colloquial way of making this point might be the phrase "first impressions count." Our first encounter with a visual form gives an instant impression and level of expectation. Once we have seen the initial visual form, we anticipate at least a part of what we expect to see or hear next. This principle can be seen at work in contemporary film, for instance, where the director can move smoothly between shots and points of view in order to establish a narrative structure, or can jump-cut to an unexpected frame in order to create elements of surprise, shock, or humor. As the linguistics theorist Roman Jakobson has stated:

the message does not and cannot supply all the meaning of the transaction, [and] . . . a good deal of what is communicated derives from the context, the code, and the means of contact. Meaning, in short, resides in the total act of communication.[1]

Audience expectation is a key factor in the development of successful design solutions and in the exploration of new forms of visual communication based on dialogue and audience interaction, themes that are explored further in **Chapter 6: Audience and Message.**

Contemporary graphic design is not always concerned with problem solving or operating in relation to a client's brief. The exploration of a theme that interests the designer and the graphic response to that theme, which might enlighten and help describe new visual languages that are applicable to other graphic solutions, is a core part of the research agenda. In effect, this places the design methodology itself as a central component of the design process. The testing and development of a visual vocabulary relevant to a specific context may then

Engaging with Visual Research

be further developed in order to address hypothetical or concrete problems within that same context. The resulting visual solutions—particularly in terms of visual form, style, and graphic conventions—can then be drawn on by the designer in relation to further practical work in the same area.

It is important at the outset, however, for the designer undertaking such a task to establish a clear set of intentions for an individual project and a critical position, relative to the subject being explored, so as to be able to reflect on progress made and to test the resulting graphic messages against a set of stated criteria—in effect, replacing the client's brief with one of the designer's own creation. The resultant design propositions are then both a combination of the personal exploration of the subject and a nascent visual language that operates within a set of predetermined objectives.

Research and Development

This shift toward an engaged and reflective practice is not in direct conflict with the traditions of commercial facilitation. Instead, the mutuality or interdependence between design experimentation and investigation and applied design thinking in a commercial sense is increased, allowing ideas of effectiveness and usefulness to inform original and propositional approaches equally. Similar approaches have been adopted within related professions: architecture, product design, advertising, branding, and marketing have all embraced quantitative and qualitative methods in order to predict potential responses and try to ensure effective outcomes. Although graphic design has touched on the same areas, the critical evaluation has been less overt, often left to the experienced eye of the designer or guided by external accounting or marketing research. As Ronald Barnett neatly summarizes:

the essential idea in this tradition in the Western university is that it is possible to critique action so as to produce more enlightened or more effective forms of action. The critical thinking in this tradition is a practice in the world, a praxis. Knowledge situated in practice is not, as is sometimes implied, a newish form of knowing alongside propositional knowledge, but is a tradition of enduring character.[2]

Critical reflection on our practice can lead to more informed judgments, the refinement of tools and techniques, and a better defined methodological framework, both for the core subject of graphic design as an academic discipline and for the wider graphic design profession.

Design and Politics

Design has long held a strong thematic association with social empowerment, from the modernist approaches of the early 20th-century pioneers to the politicized design of the post-1960s generation. Graphic designers are empowered to negotiate the visual language of everyday communication in the world around us, and as such they hold a great deal of collective responsibility. As designer and writer Andrew Howard notes, "the unique capacity of a designer is the ability to dismantle existing communication codes and to recombine some of their elements into structures which can be used to generate new narratives of the world."[3] Such narratives can persuade, surprise, reveal, or inspire—just as they can reaffirm or challenge the status quo, hold authority and convention to account, question truths, and encourage dialogue.

Such challenges are not always revolutionary. Subtle choices made by the designer in the choice of representation, color, typography, or hierarchy may lead viewers toward new ways of seeing the world around them. Design has a capacity to observe, to critique, and to reflect on the everyday—the notion of functionality or suitability of form to message is to an extent mutable, and the choices that the designer makes can help shape our world—for instance, in the rejection of negative or discriminatory stereotypes, the questioning of market-led narratives, or the proposal of innovative new tools for communication. By definition, graphic design as a form of visual communication is an inherently social activity, and as such it carries a weight of responsibility. Our world can be reshaped through the tools and practice of visual communication, and a critical perspective is vital for designers who wish to not only create effective forms of communication but also further our wider sense of knowledge and understanding.

The postmodern dilemma in all this stems from what is often termed cultural relativism—the notion that there is no fixed or correct position, that meaning is entirely contingent on context, and that all opinions on a subject might carry equal resonance. While what might be called the postmodern experiment in graphic design of the 1990s helped enormously to bring the discipline forward and to challenge established hierarchies and design conventions that certainly merited questioning, there is a sense that design education may have pushed a little too far toward uncertainty and the sense that no inherent or authoritative meanings can be understood from the long history of the profession. While empowering the reader and allowing disparate voices to be heard, the rejection of long-established and successful codes and practices has led more often than not to confusion rather than elucidation, and the relative sophistication of developed knowledge has been thrown into sharp contrast with untrained, undisciplined, and underdeveloped novelty ideas that at times have little foundation or merit.

Not only did postmodern designers dispense with any rigid adherence to formal organization and rational order, but also they seemed to throw out legibility itself. Johanna Drucker & Emily McVarish, *Graphic Design History—A Critical Guide* (2013).

In short, the construction and transmission of meaning is important, and designers hold a great deal of responsibility in relation to the continuation, or questioning, of cultural values and conventions. Acknowledging the traditional model of graphic design as a conduit for specific meanings doesn't necessarily imply a rejection of postmodern ideas of multiplicity, a range of differing interpretations, and an audience-centered approach to the content of messages. A careful balance needs to be struck between these positions in the critical understanding of visual communication. In many ways, history has come full circle, with what are sometimes termed "neomodernist" approaches gaining a foothold within graphic design. Although elements of postmodern theory and design practice have broadened the scope of the profession and allowed designers a better critical insight into the flexibility of visual language and the invisible hierarchies and power struggles implicit within such systems, many designers have begun to reappraise the value of simpler and more direct forms of communication.

1. Hawkes, T. (1997). *Structuralism and Semiotics*. Berkeley: University of California Press, 83.
2. Barnett, R. (1997). *Higher Education: A Critical Business*. Maidenhead, UK: Open University Press, 12.
3. Howard, A. (Summer 1994). "There Is Such a Thing as Society." *Eye* 13, no. 4.

Birds of a Feather

These images are a range of signs that we recognize as
denoting simple illustrations or silhouettes of a range of
species within the biological genus birds. However, they
also have individual connotations. They may indicate a
range of wild or domesticated animals, sources of food,
or rare or endangered species. They can also connote
attributes such as speed, agility, stupidity, gracefulness,
or beauty, or they might symbolize flight, wildlife, nature,
or the environment. Alternatively, they could perhaps be a
logotype for a particular corporation or a set of symbols in
a wildlife park enabling visitors to identify different animals
to be seen within that environment.

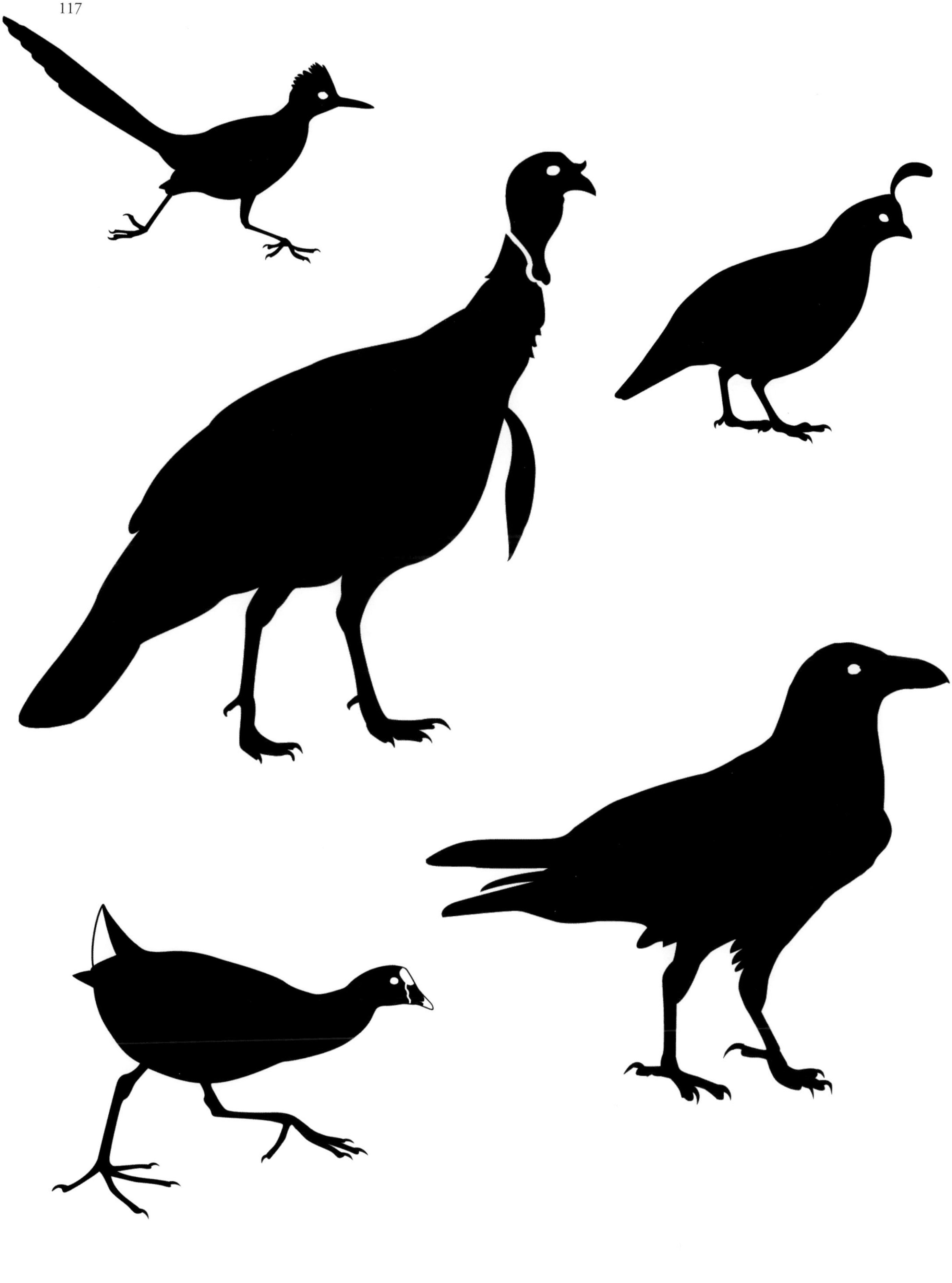

Key Concept: Modernism and Postmodernism

Modernism describes the range of art, design, and architectural movements and subsequent ideas that emerged during the first half of the 20th century, also referred to as the modern movement. In reaction to the craft movement and ideas surrounding decoration and adornment, practitioners developed a new approach that celebrated the possibilities of new technologies and methods of mass production in order to enable a better society for all. Many of the art and design movements connected to modernism, such as *De Stijl*, *constructivism*, and the *Bauhaus movement*, endeavored to celebrate functionalism and rationality under the guiding maxim that "form follows function." The modernist approach to graphic design focused on the use of white space and sans serif typography that utilized asymmetry. This was driven by an adherence to the grid, based on geometry and the proportion of the page, as a controlling device.

> *Adapting their professional practices and drawing on stylistic innovations from earlier in the century, graphic designers aligned themselves with an emerging corporate culture. Modern approaches to graphic design were distilled into a rationalist, functionalist method.*
> Johanna Drucker & Emily McVarish, *Graphic Design History—A Critical Guide* (2013).

Postmodernism is a movement that grew out of a rejection of the ideas of modernism toward the end of the 20th century. Significantly, many of the original values of modernism had, by the late 1960s, become regarded by designers as dogmatic and offering only a fixed view or superficial style. Some designers also felt that the original ideology of social progression and universal benefit that

could be derived from modernist design had to an extent been corrupted by the adoption of Swiss modernism in graphic design as the sophisticated visual language of corporate business.

Postmodernism celebrated a return to earlier ideas of the value of decoration and stylistic image-making—what Johanna Drucker and Emily McVarish describe as "decorative eclecticism." Rejecting order or discipline in favor of expression and intuition, many of the key progenitors within the field emanated originally from schools, such as Basel in Switzerland and later the Cranbrook Academy of Art in the United States, and they were tutored by central figures such as Wolfgang Weingart and Katherine and Michael McCoy. At the same time, postmodern approaches to the study of social studies, communication, and culture began to focus more closely on identity politics and the value of *difference*. Meaning within visual communication could be seen to be mutable, variable, and entirely in the mind of the reader, whose cultural background, personal identity, education, worldview, sexuality, gender, ethnicity, and self-identity were paramount.

The postmodern lexicon of historical reference, decoration, wit, and the ironic employment of vernacular or nondesigned elements, such as hand-drawn typography, constitutes a departure from the rationality of earlier approaches. This significant development brought about a reappraisal of the process of visual communication with design. Embracing ideas from architecture and 20th-century philosophy and semiotics, practitioners have attempted to advance the discussion of how relevant approaches, related to specific groups or cultures, could be developed, rather than aspiring to a universal language.

Key Concept:
Structuralism and Semiotics

According to the Swiss linguist Ferdinand de Saussure, language can be understood as a system of signs. In a series of lectures (the *Course in General Linguistics*), delivered at the beginning of the last century and published posthumously in 1915, Saussure proposed that the basic unit of any language is a *sign* or phoneme. A sign is made up of a *signifier* (an object) and a *signified* (its meaning). Similarities can be made to the twin notions of denotation and connotation (see page 70).

For example, the word *bicycle* functions in the English language by creating the concept, or signified, of a mode of transport—a machine with two wheels that is powered by its rider and that is used for traveling from point A to point B. The relationship between the signifier and the signified is arbitrary. There is no logical or natural connection between the spoken sound or graphic representation 🚲 and the concept of bicycle (this is known as duality). The connection or relationship is established solely in its use by English speakers—in the same manner that different-sounding words describe the same object in different languages: *bicyclette* (French), *bicicletta* (Italian), *Fahrrad* (German), *polkupyörä* (Finnish), *rijwiel* (Dutch), *sykkel* (Norwegian), *reihjól* (Icelandic), and so on.

Saussure was ultimately concerned with the structure (*langue*) rather than the use (parole) of language. This analytical way of thinking about the structure of language and meaning became known as *structuralism*. The basic unit of this structure, the sign, only has meaning because of its difference from other signs in the same system—the *langue*. A conceptual similarity may be made with the way that the alphabet works: individual letters are meaningless as forms in and of themselves, but they work in conjunction with other letters to present a code that can be interpreted through the act of reading.

The study of signs is also known as *semiotics*, a term coined by the American philosopher, lexicographer, and polymath Charles S. Peirce. His theories relating to language, logic, and semiotics were developed during the same period as Saussure's. Peirce was concerned with the world we inhabit and how we use language and signs to understand this world. Subsequently, the theory of semiotics was extended and developed by other writers, including Roland Barthes, Jacques Derrida, and Umberto Eco, and the theory was applied to a range of communication principles and media, including advertising, film, cognitive science, psychology, and virtual reality.

Peirce states that there are three principal kinds of signs: *iconic* signs, *indexical* signs, and *symbolic* signs. Iconic signs are likenesses that convey the idea of the thing they represent by imitating them, such as a photograph or drawing of something. These types of signs are often utilized in information design and wayfinding systems, because they offer the closest connection between an image and the object or action implied and can communicate to as wide an audience as possible. Indexical signs convey information by indicating their physical connection with the thing they represent, such as smoke to fire, or the sound of a car engine to the motion of the car. Symbolic signs are general signs that have become associated with their meanings by conventional usage, such as the colors used in traffic lights, standard practices in regard to the use of materials in editorial design, or the relative scale of type and image, for instance.

Case Study 06
Biography—The Third Truth
Designer: Colette Sadlier

Editorial designer Colette Sadlier offers a critical reflection on bibliographical writing in her research project entitled *The Third Truth: Where Myths and History Collide.* Using a biography of Sylvia Plath, *Bitter Fame* by Anne Stevenson, as a case study, Sadlier aimed to analyze the processes at work in the construction of biographical representation while also examining the nature of biography within a social, historical, political, and cultural landscape. Essentially, the aim of this project was to test the efficiency of graphic design as a critical method and to explore what it can offer biography as a discipline. As Sadlier notes:

certain parallels can be drawn between graphic design and biography, firstly in their shared lack of a central academic foundation. Still establishing as fields of study, both remain largely informed by processes and theories borrowed from other related disciplines. Graphic design, for example, often draws on theories from linguistics, semiotics or film; similarly, biography relies heavily on historiography. Additional commonalities can be found in their metadiscourse on objectivity and their aim to communicate in a way that is factual, impartial and truthful.

Biography has generally been considered to be part of historiography. By presenting itself as fact, biography allies itself with history—a history of the individual—but, as is the case with history, the facts presented to the reader have merely been selected from a myriad of facts, whereas others have been omitted according to the views and bias of the author. The biographer decides to which facts to give the floor, in what order, and in which context.

Adopting a graphic design practice-based approach to her critique of biography, Sadlier was interested in the idea of graphic authorship and the possibility of intervention by designers into the content they are working with. This meant choosing to employ similar methods to the biographical author through mediating content, experimenting with different levels of intervention, and directing the way the content is read by giving stress or emphasis to different parts of the story. The end result could be seen as a visual thesis that offers a critique of biographical representation through an analysis of the role that words, images, and the page play in the creation of meaning. The adoption of a rhetorical approach to reading, arrangement, treatment, presentation, and the visual strategies employed—contrast, irony, hyperbole, and metaphor—could be applied to any subject in order to probe the underlying processes at work or to draw attention to discrepancies and tensions within a body of research.

Plath's story has led to a great deal of interest in her life, largely because of its relevance within the context of her society. Plath is culturally significant because, as a nonfeminist living in a prefeminist era, she dramatically came to embody the cultural hardships of all women living in the patriarchal society of that time. Many women in Europe and the United States went through similar struggles as Plath did during the 1950s as they attempted to balance their evolving roles as housewives and career women, struggles that brought about the second wave of feminism in the early 1960s. Plath committed suicide, at age 30, not long after her husband Ted Hughes left her for another woman. The circumstances of her death have led to much controversy, with the finger of blame often being pointed at Hughes. To date, nearly 200 biographies of Plath have been published, offering a wide range of interpretations of her life, her character and thought processes, and her tragic

Case Study 06
Biography—The Third Truth
Designer: Colette Sadlier

demise. Published in 1989, *Bitter Fame* belongs to a different, postfeminist era. As Sadlier suggests:

The implications of this are considerable when one acknowledges that both the thought process and language used by the biographer, along with the cultural learning of the reader, mean that Plath's pre-feminist story is perceived in a postfeminist context—a context where women had been redefined by the media as strong, self-sufficient and highly achieving. Language is embedded in ideology and the language used to describe Plath in Bitter Fame *therefore carries with it the imprint of its cultural values. In the post-feminist context, when expected norms of female behaviour have moved from dependence and submission to independence and equality, Plath is dismissed as being neurotic, hysterical and responsible for her own downfall.*

It is also important to note the key part played by Plath's former husband's sister, Olwyn Hughes, in the construction of this particular biography.

Sadlier adopted a range of different graphic design techniques in her design interventions with the content of the book. These ranged from typographic reconstructions of the narrative using scale and position to highlight negative adjectives describing Plath's character to the addition of 1950s and 1960s magazine feature and advertising images depicting a then-contemporary view of female roles and stereotypes against which the text is offered as a contrast or contradiction. Employing Barthes' models of *anchorage* and *relay*, simple graphic combinations of word and image, drawing on key words and phrases in the text alongside stereotypical images of

1950s women, Sadlier was able to offer a sharp critique of the subtext of the author and the ways in which meaning was being framed by the narrative. The final output of the research embodied a book divided into three chapters. Following on from the typographic interventions and the incorporation of 1950s and 1960s imagery, Sadlier chose to create a third level of reading the text through the addition of similar images from the late 1980s and early 1990s—the period within which the book was published and in which it was therefore created to be read. Sadlier summarizes the final project as follows:

By deconstructing the content in this way, Plath's life is reduced to a series of sensationalist slogans which speak in a language reminiscent of tabloid headlines or advertising copy-lines. The graphic methodology employed by all three models of design intervention works by visually likening the heroine, "Plath," to multiple, shifting female archetypes selected from a fifty year period of history. In this sense, Plath remains elusive, as these stark alternatives work in opposition to each other by making it impossible to choose between the multiplicity of meanings and representational identities. It is this which most disturbs and fascinates about biography itself: the various possible readings and opinions about a biographical subject in the end do nothing to resolve the insoluble mystery. The "real" subject, despite being so visibly represented by others, remains hidden beneath different layers of unreliable representation, leaving us only with a commentary about the complexity of reading about and writing about, of looking and being looked upon.

RELAY

ADVANCES THE READING OF AN IMAGE BY
SUPPLYING MEANINGS THAT ARE NOT TO BE FOUND
IN THE IMAGE ITSELF. EXPLOITS THE ARBITRARINESS
OF THE RELATIONSHIP BETWEEN SIGNIFIER AND
SIGNIFIED. THE TEXT ASKS A QUESTION WITHOUT
NECESSARILY ANSWERING THAT QUESTION.

DOOMED

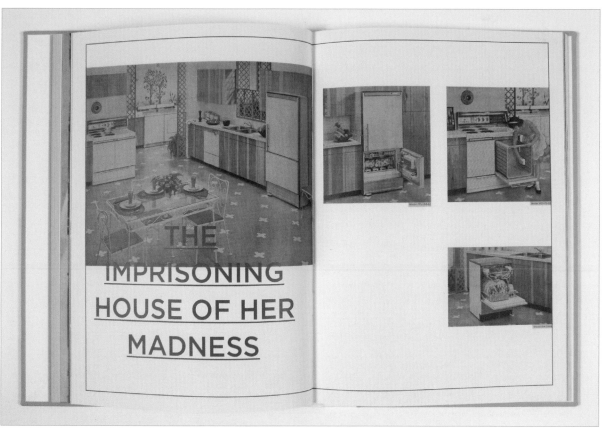

THE IMPRISONING HOUSE OF HER MADNESS

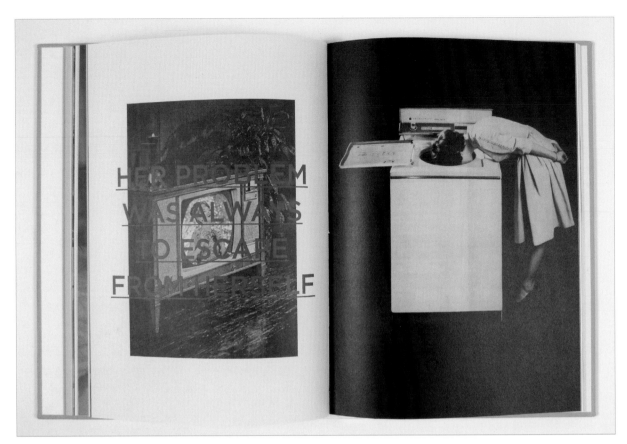

Case Study 07
Between the Lines
Designer: Alexandra Thornton

Despite technological developments in the field of electronic publishing, the long-predicted death of the traditional printed book appears as distant as ever, and as a designed object the book continues to hold a fascination for many readers and designers alike. Alexandra Thornton adopted a similar thematic investigation to Colette Sadlier's interventions into biography, although in this case the research operated at a more theoretically driven level. This involved the analysis and categorization of common styles and types of design intervention within the modern novel in the field that Thornton describes as "visual writing." Research was limited to those visual devices that exist within the lines of the typographic grid, although it also included material that draws on the effect of photographic, ephemeral, and spatial elements within this context.

As a case study model of investigation, the analytical part of Thornton's research process was based on a detailed graphic review of ten publications, all designed after the turn of the millennium. Thornton developed a methodology whereby the graphic and typographic devices were identified, analyzed, and then tested further in order to explore where visual writing may be evolving and how it might be further explored in the future as a valid branch of editorial typography and book design. In addition to this critical review of the existing context for visual writing, Thornton extended her research to include a range of practical and physical experiments extending from each of the themes identified. Existing essentially as an appendix to the thesis, this involved a series of practical graphic experiments centered on the designer's own visual writing interventions, taking as her core text the classic gothic novel *The Picture of Dorian Gray*, by Oscar Wilde.

Thornton's thesis was divided into three parts. Part One, *Probing the Narrative*, looked specifically at typographic marking and intervention and the disruption of the typographic grid, arguing that we are now more visually literate than we have ever been, and consequently we are more positioned to read books that incorporate nonstandard typographic devices. Part Two, *What We See*, studied the effect of the visual image positioned within the space of the typographic grid, and Part Three, *The Construction of the Message*, explored the way the use of space and/or graphic intervention changes the way a text is read. Thornton examined the effects of different visual devices, looking at how these might affect the reading of a text. She looked more deeply into the implication behind the premise that we are becoming more visually literate, examining visual symbolism and arguing that a more culturally intuitive understanding of the screen as a medium has also developed our perception of techniques such as framing and animation, thus positioning us to recognize these as narrative visual devices within printed matter such as books, and expanding the potential design palette accordingly. As Thornton notes:

Inherent, therefore, within the visual writing examples is the question as to whether they distract the reader from the essential message of the text, whether they can arguably be seen as a vital part of the reading process and, leading from this, whether the reading process itself is shifting and changing.

Framing the Narrative

Through a comparative analysis of the typographic and graphic design techniques employed in recent books, including Jonathan Safran Foer's *Extremely Loud &*

Conscience is the trade-name of the firm. That is all."

"I don't believe that, Harry, and I don't believe you do either. However, whatever was my motive—and it may have been pride, for I used to be very proud—I certainly struggled to the door. There, of course, I stumbled against Lady Brandon. 'You are not going to run away so soon, Mr. Hallward?' she screamed out. You know her curiously shrill voice?"

"Yes; she is a peacock in everything but beauty," said Lord Henry, pulling the daisy to bits with his long nervous fingers.

"I could not get rid of her. She brought me up to royalties, and people with stars and garters, and elderly ladies with gigantic tiaras and parrot noses. She spoke of me as her dearest friend. I had only met her once before, but she took it into her head to lionize me. I believe some picture of mine had made a great success at the time, at least had been chattered about in the penny newspapers, which is the nineteenth-century standard of immortality."

"Suddenly I found myself face to face with the young man whose personality had so strangely stirred me. We were quite close, almost touching. Our eyes met again. It was reckless of me, but I asked Lady Brandon to introduce me to him. Perhaps it was not so reckless, after all. It was simply inevitable. We would have spoken to each other without any introduction. I am sure of that. Dorian told me so afterwards. He, too, felt that we were destined to know each other."

"And how did Lady Brandon describe this wonderful young man?" asked his companion. "I know she goes in for giving a rapid precis of all her guests. I remember her bringing me up to a truculent and red-faced old gentleman covered all over with orders and ribbons, and hissing into my ear, in a tragic whisper which must have been perfectly audible to everybody in the room, the most astounding details. I simply fled".

"I like to find out people for myself. But Lady Brandon treats her guests exactly as an auctioneer treats his goods. She either explains them entirely away, or tells one everything about them except what one wants to know."

8

ONE

"Poor Lady Brandon! You are hard on her, Harry!"said Hallward listlessly.

"My dear fellow, she tried to found a salon, and only succeeded in opening a restaurant. How could I admire her? But tell me, what did she say about Mr. Dorian Gray?"

"Oh, something like, 'Charming boy—poor dear mother and I absolutely inseparable. Quite forget what he does—afraid he—doesn't do anything—oh, yes, plays the piano—or is it the violin, dear Mr. Gray?' Neither of us could help laughing, and we became friends at once."

"Laughter is not at all a bad beginning for a friendship, and it is far the best ending for one," said the young lord, plucking another daisy. Hallward shook his head.

"You don't understand what friendship is, Harry," he murmured— "or what enmity is, for that matter. You like every one; that is to say, you are indifferent to every one."

"How horribly unjust of you!" cried Lord Henry, tilting his hat back and looking up at the little clouds that,

like skeins white
   ravelled   of   glossy   turquoise   silk
were   across   hollowed
   drifting   the   sky.   of
      the   summer

Yes; horribly unjust of you. I make a great difference between people. I choose my friends for their good looks, my acquaintances for their good characters, and my enemies for their good intellects."

"A man cannot be too careful in the choice of his enemies. I have not got one who is a fool. They are all men of some intellectual power, and consequently they all appreciate me. Is that very vain of me? I think it is rather vain."

"I should think it was, Harry. But according to your category I must be merely an acquaintance."

"My dear old Basil, you are much more than an acquaintance."

"And much less than a friend. A sort of brother, I suppose?"

9

"It is not my property, Harry."

"Whose property is it?"

"Dorian's, of course," answered the painter.

"He is a very lucky fellow."

"How sad it is!" murmured Dorian Gray with his eyes still fixed upon his own portrait. "How sad it is! I shall grow old, and horrible, and dreadful. But this picture will remain always young. It will never be older than this particular day of June. . . If it were only the other way! If it were I who was to be always young, and the picture that was to grow old! For that—for that—I would give everything! Yes, there is nothing in the whole world I would not give! I would give my soul for that!"

"You would hardly care for such an arrangement, Basil," cried Lord Henry, laughing. "It would be rather hard lines on your work."

"I should object very strongly, Harry," said Hallward.

Dorian Gray turned and looked at him. "I believe you would, Basil. You like your art better than your friends. I am no more to you than a green bronze figure. Hardly as much, I dare say."

The painter stared in amazement. It was so unlike Dorian to speak like that. What had happened? He seemed quite angry. His face was flushed and his cheeks burning.

"Yes," he continued, "I am less to you than your ivory Hermes or your silver Faun. You will like them always. How long will you like me? Till I have my first wrinkle, I suppose. I know, now, that when one loses one's good looks, whatever they may be, one loses everything. Your picture has taught me that. Lord Henry Wotton is perfectly right. Youth is the only thing worth having. When I find that I am growing old, I shall kill myself."

Hallward turned pale and caught his hand. "Dorian! Dorian!" he cried, "don't talk like that. I have never had such a friend as you, and I shall never have such another. You are not jealous of material things, are you?—you who are finer than any of them!"

"I am jealous of everything whose beauty does not die. I am jealous of the portrait you have painted of me. Why should it keep what I must lose? Every moment that passes takes something from

30

me and gives something to it. Oh, if it were only the other way! If the picture could change, and I could be always what I am now! Why did you paint it? It will mock me some day—mock me horribly!" The hot tears welled into his eyes; he tore his hand away and, flinging himself on the divan, he buried his face in the cushions, as though he was praying.

"This is your doing, Harry," said the painter bitterly.

Lord Henry shrugged his shoulders. "It is the real Dorian Gray—that is all."

"It is not."

"If it is not, what have I to do with it?"

"You should have gone away when I asked you," he muttered.

"I stayed when you asked me," was Lord Henry's answer.

"Harry, I can't quarrel with my two best friends at once, but between you both you have made me hate the finest piece of work I have ever done, and I will destroy it. What is it but canvas and colour? I will not let it come across our three lives and mar them."

Dorian Gray lifted his golden head from the pillow, and with pallid face and tear-stained eyes, looked at him as he walked over to the deal painting-table that was set beneath the high curtained window. What was he doing there? His fingers were straying about among the litter of tin tubes and dry brushes, seeking for something. Yes, it was for the long palette-knife, with its thin blade of lithe steel. He had found it at last. He was going to rip up the canvas.

With a stifled sob the lad leaped from the couch and, rushing over to Hallward, tore the knife out of his hand, and flung it to the end of the studio. "Don't, Basil, don't!" he cried. "It would be murder!"

"I am glad you appreciate my work at last, Dorian," said the painter coldly when he had recovered from his surprise. "I never thought you would."

"Appreciate it? I am in love with it, Basil. It is part of myself. I feel that."

"Well, as soon as you are dry, you shall be varnished, and framed, and sent home. Then you can do what you like with yourself." And he

31

Case Study 07
Between the Lines
Designer: Alexandra Thornton

Incredibly Close (2006) and *Tree of Codes* (2010), Steven Hall's *The Raw Shark Texts* (2007), and Laurence Sterne's *The Life and Opinions of Tristram Shandy, Gentleman* (2010 edition), Thornton aimed to interrogate, define, and categorize the range of visual devices employed by different authors and designers, extrapolating this information into her own visual experiments with Wilde's *The Picture of Dorian Gray*. These devices included variations of type weight and measure, position and spacing, the addition of patterns, lines, or typographic ornaments. Further experiments included the insertion of what Thornton termed "visual metaphors" for the narrative content, together with "probing images" to guide the reader toward alternative readings of the text. These images were embedded within the text frame, rather than incorporated in a more traditional manner as illustrations, and used the principles of anchorage and relay to draw the reader toward—or away from—common readings of the text.

Thornton's final work was presented as a critical reflection on the current practice and range of visual writing, with her own understanding of each thematic set of styles and approaches further interrogated through her own practice. In this way, the work occupies something of a hybrid space, reflecting on a range of secondary graphic material and devising theoretical models and definitions to categorize that work, while attempting to engage with those approaches in a practical manner. As the designer notes:

Of great interest, however, was the realisation, through exploring and testing these forms, that there was potential for visual narratives to build up and form patterns that could not only be read, intertwined with the written ones, but could

themselves ultimately work with each other (and with the text) as a form of visual counterpoint, visually deepening, and, potentially, developing, the reading experience. It is clear here that there are screen influences that already exist within the pages of visual literature, and can continue to be developed, explored and tested. These might, ultimately, provide a bridge between the printed book and the electronic reading process.

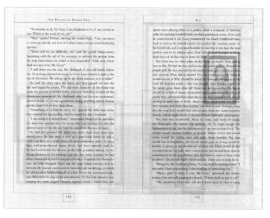
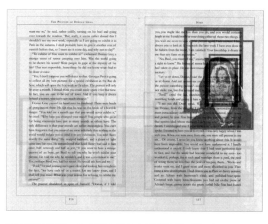
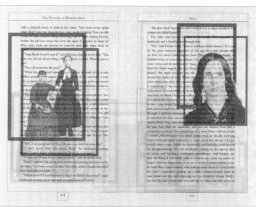
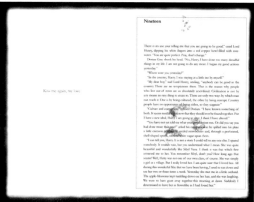
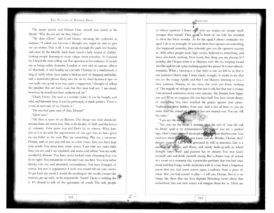

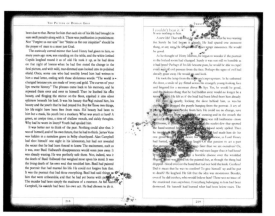
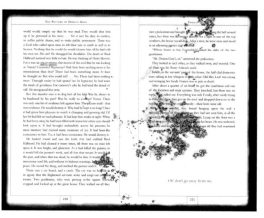

Design Activity 04: The Practice of Theory

Objective

This exercise explores how theoretical ideas can be employed to underpin design projects and design practice in general. Theory in itself has no practical application but is a useful tool for understanding. When used within design activity, it becomes part of a more strategic approach to design—what the American educator and designer Thomas Ockerse has called "principles in action." This exercise builds on the notion of visual rhetoric, in large part based on the understanding that the effective communication of an idea is closely linked to the act of persuasion.

Rhetoric traditionally encompasses a range of figures of speech, including irony, antithesis, metonymy, synecdoche, pun, metaphor, personification, and hyperbole, some of which may be utilized by the designer within visual strategies (see pages 096–099).

Gui Bonsiepe has written that pure information exists for the designer only in abstraction. As soon as he or she begins to give it concrete shape, a process of rhetorical infiltration begins.

Part 1: Visual Irony and Pun

You are asked to explore how using visual irony means you can take an existing sign—a logo, picture, or visual device—and change its meaning. A good example of this can be seen in the détournement (see page 098) of the logos and visual identities of multinational corporations, for example, by organizations such as Adbusters and those culture jammers opposed to the perceived values and activities of these companies.

Choose a company, product, or informational sign, and then begin to explore how you are able to make something that is familiar and that, to a large extent is not noticed, say something different or oppositional. This could be achieved by altering one or some of its key attributes, such as color, typeface, symbol, or image, or by changing the context or location of the sign/media. It is important that you are careful in your selection of the original media so that it is one that an audience will be familiar with in order for them to be able to appreciate its new oppositional reading. This process can also be explained by semiotics (see pages 120–121)—the relationship between what is

Key Texts

Barthes, R. (1993). *Image Music Text*. Copenhagen, Denmark: Fontana Books.

Berger, J. (2008). *Ways of Seeing*. London: Penguin Classics.

Crow, D. (2006). *Left to Right: The Cultural Shift from Words to Pictures*. Worthing, UK: AVA Publishing SA.

Crow, D. (2010). *Visible Signs: An Introduction to Semiotics*, 2nd edition. Worthing, UK: AVA Publishing SA.

Gage, J. (2000). *Colour and Meaning: Art, Science and Symbolism*. London: Thames and Hudson.

Kress, G. R. and Van Leeuwen, T. (1996). *Reading Images: The Grammar of Visual Design*. London and New York: Routledge.

Lupton, E., Abbott Miller, J. (1996). *Design Writing Research: Writing on Graphic Design*. London: Phaidon Books.

Poynor, R. (2003). *No More Rules: Graphic Design and Postmodernism*. London: Laurence King.

seen and the mental concept it produces—and the notion of connotation and denotation (see pages 070–071).

Part 2: Metaphor
You are asked to select a film or novel and produce a poster that explores how its meaning(s) or narrative ideas can be represented through the use of a visual device or series of visual items. A visual metaphor can be understood to work in a similar way to the processes at work in Part 1 of this exercise: for it to work effectively, it has to build on the understanding an audience already possesses.

Try to select a film or novel that is well known—a classic. Initially, you should explore the obvious metaphors; for example, *Romeo and Juliet* could be easily understood by the use of symbols that stand for love. You should build on this foundation to further develop your ideas to a more sophisticated level. How can other narrative subtexts be illustrated in a metaphorical manner? What can be said visually that makes a stronger and more abstract connection with the minds of the audience and their existing knowledge of the film or book? Can you

update the meaning by using a contemporary metaphor or idea, for example?

CHAPTER 06
AUDIENCE AND MESSAGE
THE RELATIONSHIP BETWEEN DESIGNER, AUDIENCE, AND MESSAGE, AND THE PRINCIPLES OF COMMUNICATION

Receiving End

Building on the communication theory precepts outlined in **Chapter 3: Analysis and Proposition**, this chapter further investigates the relationship between designer, audience, and message, and considers alternative strategies for communicating through both direct and indirect means. The production of design within a social, cultural, and political context is further explored, placing both the designer and the audience as co-participants within predefined frameworks.

In this instance, the term *social* relates to human society and its members, describing the context within which humans live together in communities or organized groups. In relation to public forms of visual communication and graphic design aimed at a broad audience demographic, social space is the realm in which interaction and communication generally takes place between individuals. The term *cultural* is more complex, however. In *Keywords*, Raymond Williams' seminal dictionary of terms used in philosophy and cultural studies, he noted that "culture is one of the two or three most complicated words in the English language."[1] The noun *culture* is often used to describe a particular society at a particular time and place, together with the attitudes and behavior that are characteristic of a particular social group or organization (often within a contemporaneous context). However, the term is extremely broad and can refer to a wide number of parallel and distinct themes, often interrelated with a range of social values and conventions. The adjective *cultural*

refers to the tastes in art and manners that are favored by a social group, often the social elite within a wider society. As such, the term can be interpreted as pejorative, describing a hierarchical position within a value system.

Any general definition of graphic design and its intentions cannot fail to make reference to communication and audience. In this regard, graphic designers could develop a vocabulary for describing and understanding their working methods through the language and theory of communication studies. Although a separate discipline with a much broader remit than graphic design, communication studies incorporates a series of useful analytical and descriptive methodologies, which relate strongly to graphic and visual communication.

Defining Audience

The term *audience* commonly refers to a group of spectators or listeners at a concert or a play, or the people reached by a book, film, radio, or television program, for instance. Within the field of graphic design, they are the recipients of a piece of communication. The audience for a visual communication outcome or product is usually clearly defined by the client in advance of the brief or, following a period of primary research, by the designer in consultation with the client. The designer obviously needs to build a clear picture of who they are attempting to communicate with, the language codes, tastes, hierarchies, sensitivities, likes, and dislikes of that group, and the

Rhetoric
Written or spoken discourse used to persuade, influence, or affect an audience.

Discourse
A body of verbal or written communication, especially between two or more participants. The act of discussion between parties, often in a formal manner.

Linguistics
The scientific study of language and its underlying structure.

reaction that the client of the message is seeking to elicit from them. That will then determine the form and the tone of the designed message.

In communication theory, the term *audiencing* refers to the ways in which readers interpret and understand texts. Research conducted into audience reading is often based on methods adopted from qualitative social science, such as interviews and ethnographic studies, together with quantitative methods based on the statistical analysis of data banks. Such studies are often centered on the interpretation of written text or the spoken word, rather than the reception of visual information. Even academic texts describing tools of visual analysis seldom focus closely on the graphic form itself, rather than the semiotic interpretation of the already constructed visual message.[2] As such, a further model for graphic designers to consider is the critical interpretation of images, with particular attention paid to the tools, materials, graphic and/or typographic elements, and formal properties of the work. Within the design process, this can often include a deconstruction of existing material (e.g., the designer evaluating the effectiveness of existing forms of communication within the same field as the brief) and a step-by-step critical reflection on the work being undertaken at each stage of the design process. Through this analysis of design methods, the designer can become more expert in the range of forms and approaches suitable for a particular context or audience.

Are You Receiving Me?

Two schools of thought exist within communication theory, the first of which might be described as the *process school*—an approach to the subject that is concerned with the actual processes of communication. This school highlights the channels and media through which messages are transmitted and by which senders and receivers encode and decode, in particular setting up a model of analysis that is concerned with matters of efficiency and accuracy. If the process of communication creates a different effect from that which is intended by the transmitter, and this in turn leads to a misreading or aberrant interpretation, then that reveals a breakdown in transmission, a flawed system or channel. This school of thought envisages a message as that which is transmitted by the communication process (and maintains that intention is a crucial factor in deciding what constitutes a message).

By contrast, the *semiotic school* is concerned with the message as a construction of signs that, through interaction with receivers, produces meaning. This school of thought views communication as an agent in the construction and exchange of meaning: by using terms like *signification* (related to the constituent parts of a message), it does not consider misunderstandings to necessarily be evidence of communication failure. Advocates for this model argue that a differing interpretation within the process of communication would validate a position more concerned with the plurality and unstable nature of messages, and with their perception of an audience dependent on culture and context. In reality, many design approaches combine both viewpoints, because the brief would normally have a clearly stated intention (e.g., to bring an audience to an event, to direct customers to service points, etc.), while an appreciation of the range of potential interpretations and an understanding of the value of audience or reader engagement can aid the creation of purposeful and interesting outcomes.

SEND

RECEIVE

Receiving End

Design is not an abstract theoretical discipline—it produces tangible artefacts, expresses social priorities and carries cultural values. Exactly whose priorities and values is at the core of the debate.
Andrew Howard, "A New Kind of Dialogue," in *Adbusters: Design Anarchy* issue (2001).

Post/Modernity

The approaches of these two schools of thought could also be applied to what are often described as the modernist and postmodernist positions within current graphic design practice and theory. The process school of graphic design—*modernity* and its legacy—is motivated by notions of universality, rationality, the clarity of communication through legibility, neutrality, and the grid. This arguably utopian worldview, based on form and functionality and a homogeneous process, could be characterized as dealing with absolutes within communication.

By contrast, what might be called *postmodern* approaches to graphic design embrace and promulgate the view of design and visual communication as an important component in the plurality of contemporary culture, and seek to emphasize its role in constructing a matrix of interpretation. Less concerned with broad bands of communication, this approach to the construction and reading of visual communication addresses specific and focused, and often smaller, communities and groups, which might be described in social, economic, or geographic terms.

The recognition that designed objects exist within a social structure, and are read by their receivers from a particular cultural perspective and subjective worldview, is central to an understanding of audience-specific graphic design. Although certain forms of graphic design may offer

some claim to the modernist objectives of universality and mass communication, much contemporary design work operates within more limited and specific boundaries. As such, a sense of familiarity with the graphic languages already understood by the target audience is crucial to the development of effective design solutions. Both qualitative and quantitative approaches are useful here, in the collection and analysis of a range of visual material operating within the same space as the intended message.

A qualitative analysis of existing artifacts and visual solutions, through the semiotic principles of connotation and denotation discussed in **Chapter 2: Design Literacy**, can help the designer to interrogate the underlying principles within effective visual messages targeting the same audience. Meanwhile, quantitative methods for reviewing and analyzing a broad range of objects in the same space, and gathering feedback from focus or survey groups, can help create a bigger picture of the range of cultural readings and messages already in place. Knowledge of existing material with which the proposed message will compete is crucial to the development of a successful design solution.

Distant Relatives

It is also important to consider the relationship between designer and client, and between client and audience, as well as that between designer, designed object, and audience. It should be noted that the designer may play only one part within the creative team involved in a project, whose members may range from marketing consultants to copywriters, programmers, and manufacturers. This area is sometimes overlooked, but the relationship and process of negotiation between client and designer is a key development in the definition of the brief. Sometimes, the

STEVE
MEDLIN
BOX 80
AREA51!
SCUM
ALIEN
BOX
Jim Loves
SUBMERGED IN DIRT
MACHINE GUN VENDETTA

Receiving End

client may be unsure of the best way to target a particular audience, or may be unclear as to the specific intentions of the message, which may be necessary to achieve a desired goal. In this case, the designer can play a central role in revising and defining the brief in order to address specific needs and provide a practical solution for the client.

Within commercial practice, the need for this kind of negotiation may mark the distinction between the context-definition and context-experiment areas of research mentioned earlier (see pages 064-065). Context-definition may be appropriate where the client has a good knowledge of their market or audience, and the brief might reflect this by being strongly prescriptive in the range of activities expected of the designer. Where the client is unsure of the specific problem to be addressed, the context-experiment model could help refine the project. In this case, the designer's initial research can help inform the direction that the project will take, and the process of negotiation between client and designer is foregrounded. Contextual research conducted by the graphic designer can both inform the client and focus the project, and will also provide a strong base on which to develop an appropriate and useful solution. It is also important to consider the role the audience plays in the construction of meaning within the context of visual communication.

Some designers have attempted to break with the traditions of the transmitter-receiver model of visual communication, either through more consultative approaches to the design (particularly in areas such as service design and transformation design), or in the creation of graphic design outcomes that offer a more open space for dialogue and interpretation to take place. Although the notion of the passive receiver of a message has been questioned within communication and language studies for many years now, it remains a fundamental principle within graphic design, both in the profession and within the academy. Through the creation of more fluid and open visual messages, the designer can attempt to engage the reader in a dialogue, to empower the receiver in the construction of meaning from within a message. By breaking the hierarchy implicit in the transmission of messages, this model could also help critique the values underpinning the message, as well as the medium through which it is transmitted, graphic design. Experiments in this field include the wide range of visual responses to the theories of poststructuralism and deconstruction, particularly those conducted at the Cranbrook Academy of Art in the United States during the mid-1990s, together with the reflexive work of politically active designers such as Jan van Toorn in the Netherlands.

Audience-Centered Graphic Design

Experiments that relate directly to communication theory can be a useful tool for graphic designers in charting alternative views of the function and purpose of visual communication, in particular those giving a greater

Icon/Iconic
Icons are likenesses that convey the idea of the thing they represent by directly resembling or imitating the signified: looking, sounding, feeling, tasting, or smelling like it.

Examples may include such items as a portrait, a cartoon, or a model.

Index/Indexical
Indexes or indications convey information by their physical

connection with the thing they represent. The signifier is not arbitrary but is directly connected in some way (physically or causally) to the signified—this link can be observed or inferred. Common examples include

smoke indicating fire, signals such as a telephone ringing or a doorbell, and pointers such as a wayfinding mark or sign.

emphasis to the receiver of the message. This way of thinking about design and communication is useful, as it allows the designer to view the reader as an active, rather than passive, participant in the process. The construction and interpretation of the message, focused in this way as an activity centered on the worldview, social, and cultural background of the receiver, can lead to a more engaged, and therefore more effective, form of communication.

Of course, this is relevant within both academic and commercial arenas: even where a commercial project attempts to target a particular market sector, an appreciation of the audience within that environment is crucial to a successful resolution. This is essential in relation to branding and identity design, where audience engagement and response is crucial to the success and longevity of the graphic message. Brand loyalty is based on far more than the graphic identity of a producer, but once an audience has bought into the range of feelings promoted within an identity, then the designer can make subtle and incremental adjustments in order to maintain a sense of exclusivity or inside knowledge in the minds of loyal customers. Within the allied fields of marketing and advertising, audience analysis and demographic studies are seen as key areas of research in the development of a project or campaign. This aspect of the creative process has become increasingly important in those areas of graphic design that attempt to address specific groups of people, such as editorial and information design, and in graphic design targeted at audiences in areas of popular culture, such as fashion and popular music.

Audience-centered graphic design covers a broad range of activities, from specific communication intended for a tightly defined target group of readers or market to attempts at empowering the receiver of the message through the employment of visual devices that reveal and display the medium, and hence highlight the communication process at work. A substantial body of work relating to audiencing and reception exists within television studies and film theory, but little work has been done in this area with regard to graphic design and the wider fields of visual communication. An examination of the ways in which readers interpret visual messages in printed form, within motion graphics on screen or via interactive displays could prove beneficial to designers and cultural theorists. Given that graphic design is largely based on very clear and specific intentions with regard to the content and context of a message, this would appear to be an area that is rich in potential for further study.

Symbol/Symbolic
Symbols are general signs that have become associated with their meanings by their use and convention, so that the relationship must be learned. Examples include spoken and written language, punctuation marks, numbers, codes, flags, and many graphic marks indicating notation or implied symbolic language to be interpreted and read by an audience that is familiar with the specific code.

1. Williams, R. (1976). *Keywords: A Vocabulary of Culture and Society.* Oxford, UK: Oxford University Press.
2. Rose, G. (2013). *Visual Methodologies: An Introduction to Researching with Visual Materials.* London: SAGE; and Barthes, R. (1993). "Rhetoric of the Image," in *Image Music Text.* New York: Hill and Wang.

Key Concept: Post-structuralism

Poststructuralism, in particular *deconstruction*, takes its starting point from the earlier ideas of structuralism proposed by Saussure and Peirce (see pages 120-121) and is significant as a theory or framework for considering the exploration of the opposition between speech and writing. The French philosopher Jacques Derrida challenges the idea that speech is regarded as more important than writing in his seminal work *Of Grammatology* (1998). Derrida states that all systems or structures have a center—a point of origin—and that all systems are constructed from binary pairs that are in relation or opposition to each other.

The focus on speech versus writing is an example of a binary system: speech = presence (physical contact between speaker and listener) and writing = absence (the written word can be read without any need for contact in time or space; we can read the words of authors who are long since departed or writers who live on the other side of the world). Speech, which is associated with presence, is traditionally favored over writing and absence. Derrida terms this *logocentrism*. These oppositions (also referred to as antonyms) exist to define each other: Good-Evil, for example, and that rather than operating separately they work together and are part of each other.

Poststructuralist ideas deny the distinction between the signifier and signified; signifiers are words that refer to other words, and their meaning is determined by one word's difference from another. The meaning of an object (the signified) is not present in this sign but in its relation to other signs. Derrida terms this *différance*. The concepts of denotation and connotation (see pages 070-071) are useful in this context. Every word or phrase has potentially two kinds of meaning: *primary*, literal meaning (denotation) and *secondary* meaning (connotation). This concept can be applied to all visual signs, and it is a particularly powerful tool in the related fields of branding and advertising.

A magazine advertisement, for example, depicting an attractive, well-dressed couple driving in an expensive-looking car may be a promotion for the clothes or jewelery they are wearing. The connotated meaning may suggest that purchasing one of these items is the key to achieving a happy life and a successful career, to owning an expensive car, and to having a relationship with an attractive partner. The context of this advertisement in a consumer or lifestyle magazine and our experiences and cultural background will have an impact on how we read the image and our relationship to its coded messages. From a more critical perspective, the image may connote cultural standards that the reader chooses to question or reject, for environmental, ecological, ideological, or political reasons—for instance, the rejection of consumerist culture, environmentally damaging forms of transport, or stereotypical modes of dress and presentation. The meaning of the representation and how we read it is not fixed by its creator or author but is equally determined by the reader.

Key Concept:
Memes and Fitness Landscapes

Meme theory, or memetics, is a theory of cultural development that draws on genetic models of biological evolution in order to explain the transfer and propagation of so-called good ideas within social or cultural groups. Memes (ideas, belief systems, and patterns of behavior) can be conceptualized in a similar manner to genes within evolutionary theory. Memes can replicate and are passed on between individuals, although in this case the vehicle for such transfers is within shared cultural groups, rather than through biological reproduction. Within this analogy, trends, beliefs, fashions, and linguistic phrases are passed from generation to generation and through social groups among a process of imitation and behavioral replication, in a similar manner to models of biological evolution and genetic adaptation. Human cultures then evolve via contagious communications in a manner similar to the evolutionary development of the gene pool of species over time.

The term *memetics* was first coined by Richard Dawkins in his 1976 book *The Selfish Gene*, a hugely influential text on evolution from the perspective of the fundamental needs of genetic reproduction, which went some way to explain certain human and animal traits and characteristics as products of the genetic survival mechanism. Memes, in Dawkins' terms, were theoretical replicators of cultural evolution, which acted in a similar manner to biological genetics and were intertwined in survival instincts among social groups and individuals within the same species. The theory has been further developed to explain technological, linguistic, cultural, and social evolution, the potential for artificial intelligence in computers, and even the spread of religious belief by other writers, notably Daniel Dennett and Aaron Lynch.

Fitness landscapes are used as conceptual models to demonstrate relative strengths and weaknesses in the gene pool. The concept of the "survival of the fittest" design idea is actually better modeled as a landscape of peaks and troughs, with the best ideas higher up the slopes and those that will die at birth, or that are unlikely to survive, further down in the valleys.

This model shows that evolution is not about a single perfect answer that resides on the peak of the mountain (where the perfect example of the species might get struck by lightning or die some other unfortunate death), but a range of iterations that follow a contour around the higher reaches of the slopes. This indicates a good analogy for design as an iterative process, with the potential for many alternative paths to follow and potential solutions to a problem. There may be no single perfect answer, but there are both better, and worse, solutions to the brief, and there is usually more than one way to guide the reader toward a preferred reading.

Case Study 08
Mapping Meaning
Designer: Alison Barnes

Maps are an accepted part of everyday life and, for most people, they are simply a graphic representation of space, regardless of whether they deal with road systems, populations, or natural features of the landscape. They have become embedded in society as an unquestioned truth, a reality; they have become the territory. However, the territory, its inhabitants, and their behaviors are inevitably more complex than conventional maps illustrate. Information design is an important process in the editing, analysis, and successful visual communication of content. The designer can collect information and treat it in such a way as to emphasize new meaning that may be inherent in familiar content. Mapping, the systematic organization of complex information in a form that may be transported and reinterpreted, is an activity that has much in common with graphic design; the collecting, editing, and representation of information in a communicable visual form might be defined as the very core of the discipline. Designers have a responsibility to create work that is both accessible and understandable to its intended audience. As such, it is essential that research is conducted into the target audience for a particular message in order to ascertain the quality and appropriateness of materials used and visual language adopted, together with the range of contexts within which the work might be viewed and interpreted.

Designer and educator Alison Barnes used the tools of the cartographer and the information designer within this project, originally published in the first edition of *Visual Research*, which attempted to investigate the human dimension that is often lacking within traditional forms of urban mapping such as street maps. Although one might expect to find details of historically or culturally important locations, together with street names and navigational devices, on any given town map, Barnes was interested in displaying alternative visual signs that demonstrated human intervention and the traces of its use as both a social and an architectural space. Her maps, detailing alternative views of the area of New Basford in Nottingham, England, chart the more familiar aspects of modern urban spaces, such as graffiti and historical changes of use within specific buildings—for example, brownfield site developments, the renovation of industrial and commercial buildings for residential or social use, and the changes in denomination of religious and secular buildings.

By limiting the information displayed on each map in the series, particular emphasis was given to those aspects of the area that are usually unnoticed in Ordnance Survey and town street maps: such details included the number of trees and public green spaces, or elements of brick decoration that mark sections of streets built by the same builders within the same period. Drawing on wide-ranging theories from the Situationists (the 1960s avant-garde art movement whose models of psychogeography were both an art practice and a political statement), together with those from sociology, geography, architecture, and design, Barnes endeavored to develop a methodology for mapping everyday life and space; to create maps of meaning rather than "skeletal landscapes of statistics."

One striking implication of this method is the possibility for the viewer to combine maps that give specific information in order to read the interrelationship between the two: the relationship between green areas, parks, or trees and instances of graffiti, for example. Barnes is careful not to guide the reader toward specific conclusions that might be drawn from this exercise.

The emphasis is always on the social use of the space, rather than its simple physical features. This notion of a human geography is particularly important within one map in the series, which is based on the oral testimony of four elderly people living in a local residential home. Barnes interviewed them and documented their memories of the places where they used to live, work, and socialize. The resulting color-coded map shows the locations that each person described, and allows the reader to interpret any overlaps in those places used as social space (e.g., work, shopping, or leisure), together with those that might be described as personal spaces (e.g., homes, gardens, and birthplaces).

Barnes asked: "can it ever be possible to really map a space, reflect the true nature of the landscape (clearly this implies something more than just physical representation) and convey a real sense of the everyday life of users of that space?" Electing to analyze the range of vernacular and low-tech signs of the area such as graffiti, Barnes systematically documented the signs of each street to produce a range of topographical maps of the area. The term *vernacular* in this context refers to the study of nondesigned typography such as graffiti as a valuable source of information about our culture. This detailed plan for the project allowed her to investigate a wide range of overlapping themes, while relating them to each other in the project methodology. The central base map could be described as closest to a standard street map, as it detailed architectural spaces, highways, public, and residential buildings. However, even here there was room for alternative approaches. Barnes's maps of residential and commercial property included color-coded diagrams of the age of the buildings and information about changes in use, for instance, the conversion from light industrial and factory sites to housing and retail spaces. When combined with information about graffiti or oral histories, a far more complex and human picture of the environment can be developed in the reader's mind.

This approach to the use of the tools of visual communication and information design has been described as visual journalism, indicating how graphic design can be applied not only to wider social situations but also to a personal position regarding the role and function of the graphic designer. The traditional roles of the designer remain, but new debates and discussions within the profession are beginning to offer possibilities for designers to explore more personal interests and reflections within their work.

Critical Reflections:—An Interview with the Designer

With more than fifteen years of experience in teaching graphic design in the United Kingdom and Australia, Alison's practice-led research continues to focus on everyday life and place, drawing on both graphic design and cultural geography. Her most recent project focuses on the relationship between migrants' material and imaginative home-making practices and how these multisensory experiences might be understood and represented via creative methods.

After undertaking this project, how was the outcome received, by academic and/or professional audiences?
The project was received very well, as it draws on both graphic design and cultural geography theory and practice, and it has been disseminated successfully in both academic disciplines. The discussions with geographers were the most exciting for me, as this began to really open up the opportunity for interdisciplinary work.

Case Study 08
Mapping Meaning
Designer: Alison Barnes

Many contemporary geographers are turning to "creative methods" to understand and represent place, so my work was timely in that respect.

How has your subsequent career developed?

My interest in cultural geography began with this work, and the MA made me realize that I wanted to develop my ideas further through a PhD. Having this work as a foundation meant I was in an excellent position to draft a clear proposal. Since the successful completion of this, my work has been presented and published internationally, and I have been lucky enough to work as a graphic design lecturer at the University of Western Sydney in Australia for the past three years.

How do you now feel about the methods developed within this project? Have you applied them or extended any further in your own personal practice or professional work?

While I think the project still has a lot of merit, looking back, I feel I was working through it mostly on instinct, not really understanding that there was a much bigger body of practice or theory—for example, around ethnographic methods—that I could have located the work within or drawn from. However, with that said, I still feel the detail drawn from the infra-ordinary, everyday elements that more often than not go almost unnoticed within place, such as the scribbles of low-level graffiti, allowed me to understand and reveal the spatial practices of the local residents or users of that place that would otherwise remain hidden. This aspect of the everyday has remained crucial to my work as it has developed further, and mapping and documenting place, often using participatory methods, is still critical to my practice.

What other elements do you feel could or should be considered when undertaking a similar project—on reflection, how would you change or refine the process?

The form of the map itself can be critiqued, as maps position everything on the same plane, in the same time zone, regardless of night and day, playing what is called the "god trick," allowing us to see places from above, giving us a somewhat removed, but seemingly objective, overview. I prefer to view maps in a more dynamic way, remade each time they are engaged with, with the series of points, lines, and shaded areas requiring the map-reader to bring them to life. One of the issues one has to contend with in work about the everyday is that contemporary definitions of place position it as ongoing and relational; always in flux and, therefore, never finished. To this end, many cultural geographers have begun to explore media such as film or sound, perceiving these to be less fixed than print-based work. However, I firmly believe that print can engage the reader in such a way as to give a nonlinear or interactive experience.

The maps in this case were printed on translucent stock, so that they could be overlaid to reveal connections and contradictions to be interpreted by the user, thus bringing them to life. In a way, the work isn't about mapping at all, it is about storytelling. In more recent work, I have pushed further the idea of what a map might be and produced experimental books that allow the reader to chart quite individual journeys through the content; via typography and layout, and via form, structure, and media. Pushing the boundaries of what some might consider a dated media, unsuited to current notions of place, has developed my practice in ways I wouldn't have anticipated, but I think this is one of the joys of drawing on interdisciplinary thinking—it can challenge your thinking and lead to unexpected results.

Topophilia in New Basford

This map shows the levels of topophilia
within the area. The word topophilia is the
result of combining two Greek words to mean
'love of place.' Individuals have an emotional
need to identify with often personal and intimate
places, and hence 'construct' these places for
themselves. Each house has been assessed
and marked on four elements: the overall
condition of paintwork, the front door (house
number, letterbox, door knob, etc), the windows
(net curtains, ornaments, etc) and the garden or
street at the front. The marking system was as
follows: 20 excellent, 15 good, 10 average,
5 poor, 0 very poor

Key

65 +	55 – 60	45 – 50	35 – 40	25 – 30	15 – 20	0 – 10	Garden/yard	Property not assessed

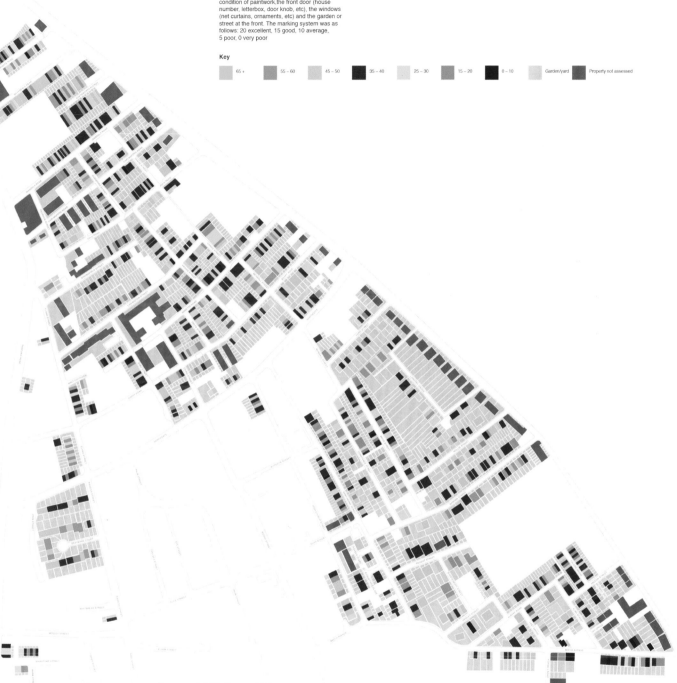

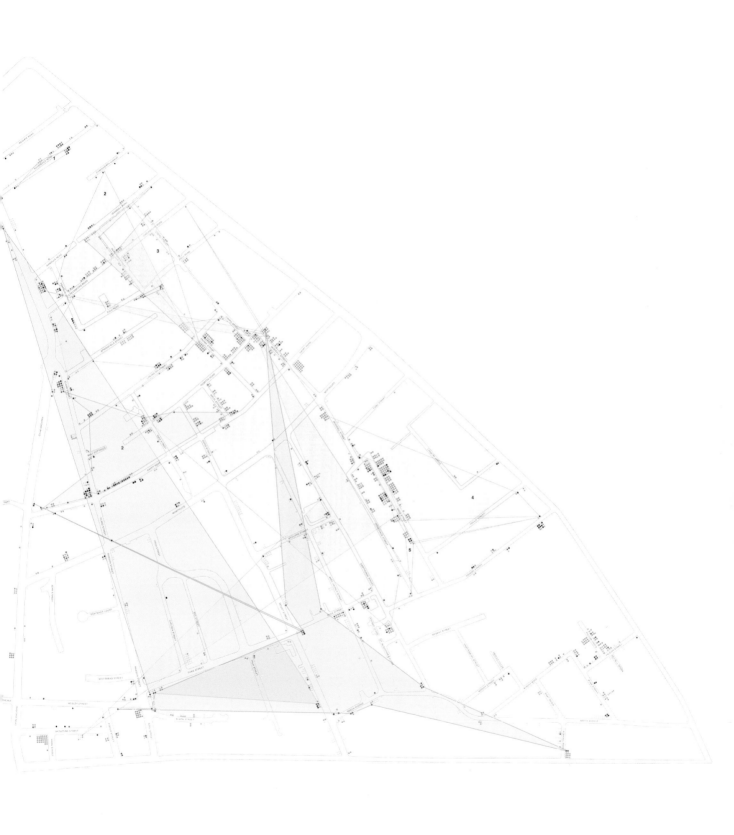

Albany Road

Alma Street

Foxhall Road

Gawthorne Street

   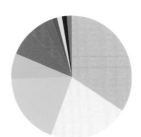

Chatsworth Avenue **Chelsea Street** **Delta Street** **Duke Street**

Brick decoration in New Basford

This map shows all brick and ceramic tile
decoration on the houses within the area.
The decoration is mapped in place of the
house it appears on. The representations
are not exactly to scale.

Key

■ Brick decoration

▨ Ceramic tile

Case Study 09
Tirez Magazine
Designer: Amy Cooper-Wright

Designing material in a foreign language can be a complex task for a graphic designer. Producing a magazine in one language that is aimed at an audience who use a different language complicates things even further. Editorial designer Amy Cooper-Wright chose to develop a personal project based on her own experience as a fluent speaker of French as a foreign language, with a keen interest in French culture. Cooper-Wright observed that there has been a steep decline in the study of modern languages in British schools, noting "a nationwide ambivalence to language-learning in general, and a lack of enthusiasm towards our nearest neighbours to whom we owe over fifty percent of our own mother tongue." She also noted that the French language was used in many countries and regions around the world, and that this offered a rich resource for visual content that could appeal to a wide range of interested readers.

Cooper-Wright started her investigation with an open-ended research question: How can the French foreign-language learning tool be redesigned in order to make the subject more relevant and engaging to a British audience? Through consultation with a range of respondents to her initial surveys on the subject, she found that the French language is overwhelmingly associated with the school classroom. Cooper-Wright noted that many British people do not naturally consider it outside of that context, and that the process has for too long focused on exams and school qualifications, rather than a real-world engagement with and enjoyment of the language. Her working methodology involved the creation of a range of bilingual and French-language-only graphic material that was intended to engage an English-speaking audience through its form and content, while offering a learning experience:

By relocating the subject within a new genre, the language learner can begin a process of meaningful, situated learning. The process becomes a journey of discovery, and acquisition of knowledge as an integral part of experience, rather than the receipt of knowledge for its own sake.

The proposed target audience for the work was British adults of any age, who may have learned French to some extent at school but who in many cases had become disengaged from the language. Through the adoption of a lifestyle magazine format, Cooper-Wright aimed to create opportunities for the reader to interact with words and images about a French-speaking place:

The proposition for the magazine is: a bilingual magazine about the French-speaking world. Whilst there is an educational element central to the project, it should introduce itself as a magazine, not a textbook. The magazine should feel accessible and friendly, to encourage people to give it a try; it must be current and of course it should feel French. At the same time, it must be authoritative so that the information is trusted, without feeling overly academic.

Her first set of experiments involved the typographic layout of two parallel texts, containing the same information in English and French. Dual-language texts have been presented side-by-side since Roman times, offering the reader the opportunity to scrutinize the translation. This approach is often used as a method for learning to read in a foreign language, allowing cross-referencing, although the designer found sentence construction and functionality proved problematic,

THE BILINGUAL MAGAZINE ABOUT THE FRENCH-SPEAKING WORLD

Entrance to Le
Corbusier's *Maison
du Brésil* in the Cité
Universitaire, Paris 14e

7

Case Study 09
Tirez Magazine
Designer: Amy Cooper-Wright

together with the lack of images or illustration frustrating some readers. Her next chosen method was more illustrative. Historically, dictionaries and encyclopedias included illustrations, and this method is successfully employed today in learning tools aimed at children. This represents something much closer to the Saussurean model of signifier and signified, connecting an object with a word to denote it. Cooper-Wright asserts that "Too often in language learning tools aimed at adults, we see a reliance on word-only lists. It would be more appropriate to pair the French signifier with the signified (and omit the English word from the equation)."

Initial attempts to find a theme that could be the subject matter for the publication proved to be a challenge. Cooper-Wright considered a range of topics, from the predictable (French cooking, film, cycling) to the more contemporary (French rap, parkour). She was reluctant to make a statement about what Frenchness is or is not, or to cater to a niche market, so she settled on a different approach—to be an unbiased observer, to capture a multifaceted view of life in each location depicted in the stories. This then led to the decision to make the series of magazines all about French-speaking cities. An opportunity to cover all corners of the francophone world, this would raise awareness of the fifty or so countries and states besides France in which people speak French. It would also provide interesting new content for each issue. The proposal was that an editorial team would travel to a new city each time to carry out the research for that particular issue. It would create a sense of anticipation if the magazine gained a readership, where readers would look forward to the next issue.

After exploring several naming routes, the designer settled on *Tirez*, which means "pull" and can also mean

"shoot" or "print." When spelled Tirez it is the imperative form, as in "Pull!" As Cooper-Wright asserts:

This is a provocative call to action, i.e., pick up the magazine and read it. The logo is designed to reference the door signs in public buildings all over France, in the hope that the audience may recognise this and so understand the word by knowing the context (a central theme of the project). It is also telling them to "open the door," i.e., open the cover of the magazine, and in a figurative sense to open the door to a new experience of language learning.

A series of draft dummy magazines were produced, with an indicative range of covers and locations for further issues in the series. The final outcome takes the form of a proposal with designed visuals, rather than a fully formed set of products. Cooper-Wright also devised a digital model of the magazine for the iPad or e-reader, whereby a more complex system of revealing and translating words could be utilized in order to vary the content and encourage user interaction.

159

Welcome   Bienvenue

to the first issue of *Tirez*, the magazine that offers a more engaging way to brush up on your French, whilst getting to know the *francophone* world...

au premier numéro de *Tirez*, la magazine qui vous offre un moyen plus engageant de se remettre à son français, tout en faisant conaissance du monde *francophone*...

50 PARIS 2012
Photo essay, charting moments of the
everyday in Paris, on a weekend in June

The Paris Issue

Each issue of *Tirez* is produced in a different French-speaking city spanning the full extent of the *francophone* world. But before we jet off, this first issue takes a fresh look at a city we thought we knew so well...

28 DEGAGE COLLECTF
Support for the Tunisian Revolution, denoted by the word
"Degagé" here adorned on a building in Paris

In Britain we are bombarded with stereotypes about Parisians – sitting around pouting all day and smoking Gitanes. It is true, of course, that some do, but then there are Londoners who take high tea at 3pm while the rest of us live more modern lives.

This fresh look at Paris is the result of spending time with locals and wandering about their city with them. It was in these unassuming streets, far from the Champs-Elysée and the horde of tourists, that we encountered statements of support for the Arab Spring painted in beautiful typography on an abandoned building (p.28); the textures (p.96) and colours (p.12) of the city streets that reveal a deeply ingrained Parisian style, the faces of the children in the park (p.50). These coincidental, unremarkable observations make up an honest portrait of the city.

AMY WRIGHT, EDITOR

En Grande Bretagne, on nous bombarde de stéréotypes par rapport aux Parisiens – restez assis toute la journée en faisant la moue et en fumant des Gitanes. C'est vrai, bien sûr, qu'il y en a, mais il y a aussi des Londoniens qui prennent le thé à 15h pendant que le reste vit une vie plus moderne.

Cette perspective fraîche de Paris est le résultat d'avoir passé du temps avec les gens du coin et de flâner avec eux. C'était dans ces rues sans prétentions, loin des Champs-Elysée et de la horde de touristes, que nous voyons concentrée des déclarations d'appui au Printemps Arabe, peint en belle typographie sur le côté d'un bâtiment abandonnée (p.28); les textures (p.96) et les couleurs (p.12) des rues qui révèlent un style Parisien bien enraciné, le visage de l'enfant au parc (p.50). Ces observations quotisonnaires, de coincidence, font un portrait honnête de la ville.

AMY WRIGHT, RÉDACTRICE

94 EN-DESSOUS DE VOS PIEDS
Textures beneath your feet

l'herbe verte

12 LA VILLE PAR COULEURS
A photo essay focusing on the colours that make Paris unique, presented in the form of an illustrated dictionary.

78 ORIANE TELLE
Interview with a young Martinican living in Paris

92 LIVRES RECOMMANDÉS
Recommended read: Paris vs. New York

94 LES NOUVELLES
French press of the past 3 months

92 FILMS RECOMMANDÉS
Film choice

PATRIMOINE MONDIAL DE L'HUMANITÉ

106 PROGRAMME PARIS
Comprehensive Paris listings

38 PHILIPPE APELOIG
The Parisian graphic designed, world renowned for his poster design and typographic illustrations.

HOW IT WORKS
Tirez is a bit different – it is a magazine, but it is also a way of brushing up on your French. We aim to do this in a way that's fun and focused around articles and features, with lots of images to help.

LOOK AT THE PICTURES
We all remember learning to read as kids and using the pictures to work out what the words say. Well, here it is a similar idea but the stories are a bit more grown-up.

CROSS REFERENCE
Many of the articles have the English and a French text side-by-pice. We have highlighted key words to help you keep track – try reading them together.

DON'T DESPAIR
You will find that you do not understand every word, but don't worry. You will absorb new words over time and learn as much from the pictures as the text – after all it is just as important to learn about the places where French is spoken, as it is to learn new words.

READ THE SMALL PRINT
We have often put headlines in French, but if you read the accompanying captions, they should help you work out what it's all about.

LOOK FOR FAMILIAR WORDS
Over 30% of the English language is derived from French, so if you look out for familiar words you will spot many with the same or similar spelling to their English equivalents.

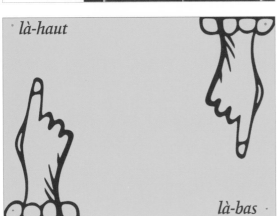

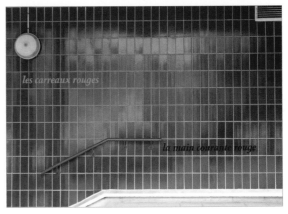

EDITORIAL | DÉGAGE

"Dégage" is the name of a group of Tunisian photographers who, under the supervision of the curator, Mrs Souissi Leila, offers an itinerant exhibition in homage to the Tunisian revolution. This exhibition, which was shown at the Institut du Monde Arabe in Paris (IMA, may 19- 29, 2013), is scheduled in various countries such as Germany, Italy, Belgium, France, Turkey…and of course everywhere in Tunisia.

The Dégage Collective is a group of francophone photographers, who created an exhibition paying witness to the days of violence that took place during the Arab Spring of 2011 in Tunisia. As a means to raise awareness of the exhibition, they adorned abandoned buildings around Paris with the word Dégage.

Previous page:
Extract from Le Nouvel Observateur, February 2012.

This page:
Extract from Leila Souissi, Collectif Dégage (http://www.myspace.com/collectifdegage). **Photography** © Amy Wright, Paris, June 2012.

DICTIONNAIRE

NB. TIREZ! IS THE IMPERATIVE OF TIRER, AS IN "PULL!"

DICTIONARY

TIRER (tire)

[a] TRANSITIVE VERB

(pour arracher, amener à soi) to pull. Il m'a tiré les cheveux • He pulled my hair. Tiré par les cheveux (FIGURATIVE) (histoire, intrigue, explication) far-fetched

(to fermer) (volet, porte, tiroir) to pull to, to close (> rideau) to draw tirer les rideaux • to draw the curtains

(to extraire) tirer qch qch to take sth from sth, to pull sth out of sth (> front, sol) to extract sth from sth. Elle a tiré un mouchoir de son sac. • She took a handkerchief from her bag, She pulled a handkerchief out of her bag tirer son nom de to take one's name from, to get one's name from tirer qch de qn to get sth out of sb tirer qn de (> conserver) to help sb out of sth, to get sb out of sth tirer qn d'embarras to get sb out of an awkward situation tirer qn d'un mauvais pas to get sb out of a fix

(> sortir) tirer la langue to stick out one's tongue (bien que arme) (> balle, coup de feu) to fire (> pistolet) to shoot il a tiré plusieurs coups de feu. He fired several shots (> blessé) to draw

(> tracer) to draw, to trace tirer un trait to draw a line tirer un trait sur qch (FIGURATIVE) to draw a line under sth tirer un trait sur son passé to draw a line under one's past

(> imprimer) (> journal, livre, photo) to print

(> choisir) (> carte) to draw tirer les cartes to read the cards, to tell the cards tirer au sort to draw lots tirer des conclusions to draw conclusions

[football] (> corner) to take

(marine) tirer 6 metres to draw 6 metres of water

[b] INTRANSITIVE VERB

tirer sur qch (> corde, poignée) to pull on sth, to pull at sth (> pipe) to draw on sth

(avec arme) to shoot (> bête tué) to shoot, to fire tirer à l'arc to shoot with a bow and arrow tirer à la carabine to shoot with a rifle, to fire with a rifle tirer sur qn (> tirer feu sur) to shoot at sb, to fire on sb il a tiré sur les policiers He shot at police officers, He fired on police officers

[football] to shoot

(durer/to) to draw tirer à sa fin to be drawing to an end tirer en longueur to drag on

Dictionnaire

IT IS BETTER TO LEARN ONE WORD, THAN TO FORGET TWENTY! SO EACH ISSUE, WE WILL GIVE YOU ONE NEW WORD, WITH AN ILLUSTRATION OF THE CONTEXT IN WHICH IT CAN BE USED. AND WHERE BETTER TO START THAN WITH OUR NAME – TIREZ!

Design Activity 05: Are You Receiving Me?

Objective

The intention of this project is to encourage you to explore the relationship between the word and the image and how, when working in combination, a wide range of communication ideas can be explored. This project uses photography as its basis.

Part 1: Collecting Images
Working in groups of three, you should produce or collect images that address the following:
• Three images of yourself or yourselves as a group
• Three images of objects that relate to you
• Three images of the environment that you live in and that relates to you

All images should be printed out at A4/Letter size in full color. Try to create images that are photographed in an objective or neutral documentary style. These images form the foundations for Part 2.

Part 2: Building a Lexicon
You should now build a set of individual words that relate to yourself and the environment in which you live. These words should not be captions to the images you have created but should be words that have potential multiple meanings for the reader; they might relate to the meaning or context of the images but should not describe the images specifically. Try to build a lexicon of words without referring directly to the work done in Part 1 of the brief. It may be useful to select a theme on which to base this spoken or textual language.

Part 3: Word/Image Relationships
Begin to place the words and images together. Try to look at a wide range of variations and possibilities. The intention here is to find word/image relationships that have possible multiple readings—words that unlock meaning in the images—not words that close down the number of possible readings that each combination may produce.

Key Texts

Barthes, R. (2009). *Mythologies*. London: Vintage Classics.

Baxandall, M. (1987). *Patterns of Intention: On the Historical Explanation of Pictures*. New Haven, CT: Yale University Press.

Buchanan, R. & Margolin, V. (1995). *Discovering Design: Explorations in Design Studies*. Chicago: University of Chicago Press.

Crow, D. (2010). *Visible Signs: An Introduction to Semiotics in the Visual Arts*, 2nd edition. Worthing, UK: AVA Publishing SA.

Emmison, M. & Smith, P. (2000). *Researching the Visual: Introducing Qualitative Methods*. London: SAGE.

Hawkes, T. (1977). *Structuralism and Semiotics*. London: Methuen.

Norman, D. A. (2002). *The Design of Everyday Things*. New York: Basic Books.

Pevsner, N. (1946). *Visual Pleasures From Everyday Things: An Attempt to Establish Criteria By Which the Aesthetic Qualities of Design Can Be Judged*. London: B. T. Batsford.

Poynor, R. (2003). *No More Rules: Graphic Design and Postmodernism*. London: Laurence King.

Rose, G. (2007). *Visual Methodologies: An Introduction to the Interpretation of Visual Material*. London: SAGE.

Part 4: Word/Image Combinations

Once you have decided on the most effective word/image combinations, consider how to place the type within or on the image so that both can be read without disturbing the effect of each other. Try to consider a typeface that is not too decorative, and avoid fonts that may distract from the image. This font should be employed for each word on each of the images. You should try to find a common format and scale for each of the images so that a degree of consistency exists among them and so they can be read as part of a larger set or family.

Part 5: Arrangement

Once this task is completed, begin to arrange the word/image combinations in sequences that create possible narratives. Try to consider the multiple reading of each individual word/image combination, as well as the overall readings the combined narrative may create.

This process asks you to consider how as a designer you can use image and word/type to create open and multiple readings for an audience. This should be undertaken with the widest possible audience in mind for the work. You should try to consider the scope of potential readings dependent on key factors such as background, age, education, and culture. Each and all of these elements are essential considerations for the designer, and they should be a central part of your approach when thinking about how messages are communicated and, importantly, understood.

CHAPTER 07
PROCESS AND MATERIALS

EXPERIMENTATION WITHIN THE DESIGN STUDIO: SYSTEMATIC APPROACHES TO THE PRODUCTION OF PRACTICAL WORK AND PHYSICAL FORM

Practical Considerations

This chapter deals with the notion of systematic approaches and experimentation within the design studio through the production of practical work. Materials investigation is explored, within the professional arena, through the testing of appropriate form relative to a consistently applied set of criteria, and as a process in itself in the exploration of new and innovative visual languages appropriate to specific audiences or circumstances. This reflective process might be described as "research into design"—the exploration of design methods and practices, including visual testing and experimentation with materials and the potential of physical form.

Many creative disciplines within the visual arts arena place a great deal of emphasis on surface and materials—the plasticity of the image. In the field of fine arts, within areas such as painting and sculpture, for instance, the base materials used in the construction of the work (e.g., oil paints, acrylics, watercolors, pastels, bronze, stone) are crucial to the reading and understanding of that work. Similarly, photographs carry meaning through their material nature and also the context within which they are displayed: on a wall in a gallery or home, in a family album, within an archive, or more typically nowadays, on a screen, tablet, or mobile phone. The physical interface between image and viewer is essential in the construction and interpretation of meaning.

One key difference with the disciplines of film and photography, however, lies within the nature of the image itself. The realism of the photographic image, particularly through the use of color film or moving image, can lead the viewer to read the content of the image—the scene depicted—but ignore its materiality (factors such as photographic paper, borders, mounts and frames, the physical presence of the screen or projected image). As Elizabeth Edwards and Janice Hart suggest:

> *The prevailing tendency is that photographs are apprehended in one visual act, absorbing image and object together, yet privileging the former. Photographs thus become detached from their physical properties and consequently from the functional context of a materiality that is glossed merely as a neutral support for images.*[1]

Where the material nature of the photograph does take primacy, it is usually within the field of the fine print or in regard to conservation and the longevity of the physical support.

Materials and Materiality

The term *materiality* relates to the physical properties and qualities of an object. In relation to graphic design, this might mean the physical nature of a book, for example; how it is printed, its binding, the materials it is constructed from, its size, mass, and volume, texture, paper thickness or stiffness, and its status as an object

---

Tactility
Perceptible to the sense of touch. Surfaces and objects can be described as tactile when they are designed to be felt, rather than purely seen or heard.

Tangibility
Capable of being touched or felt, having real material substance. This may also be extended to the outward perception or appearance of having tactility or substance.

Texture
The visual and especially tactile quality of a surface. Texture relates to the properties held and sensations caused by the external surface of objects arising from the sense of touch. Texture can also be used to describe a pattern that has been scaled down to the point where the individual elements that go on to make the pattern are not distinguishable.

beyond its content and functionality as a form of communication. An approach to design that focused on materiality would encompass the relationship of the physical properties of the book to its intended audience and the relevance of how it is presented as a whole. This aspect of design is sometimes referred to as the plastic or plastique of an object, in relation to the combination of several elements into a whole. With reference to the visual arts in general, the term is derived from the phrase "plastic arts," in particular referring to three-dimensional art, such as sculpture. In the context of graphic design, materiality or plasticity can also refer to an activity where there is no physical object present, including screen-based, interactive, and virtual environments such as the Internet or cyberspace.

Another consideration in regard to materials relates to *durability*—the capacity of an object to withstand wear and tear or decay. This includes the capacity to continue to be useful or purposeful after an extended period of time and usage, and the power of resisting agents or influences that tend to cause changes, decay, or dissolution. In relation to graphic design, these elements might include physical handling, heat, light, or compression, and durability describes the manner in which the material surface withstands fading, tearing, distortion, or corruption that might disrupt the reading of the design.

Graphic design . . . forms the connective tissue that holds so many ordinary visual experiences together. We don't usually view a professional photograph in isolation: we view it as part of a page, screen, billboard, or shop window display in relationship with other pictorial, typographic and structural elements determined in the design process. These frameworks and relationships are an indivisible part of the meaning.
Rick Poynor, "Out of the Studio: Graphic Design History and Visual Studies," *Design Observer* (2011).

Art and Craft

Graphic design, particularly in the printed form, lies somewhere between artistic craft or mark-making and photographic realism. It lacks the supposed neutrality or transparency of the photographic image, but still usually foregrounds the internal message—the content—rather than the surface material as the central conveyor of meaning. This is especially true in the form of the book, where traditionally a typographer would strive for clarity of reading *through* the typographic layout and grid structure. At the same time, the surface is usually clearly evident, as printed material or in the thickness and volume of a bound book, for instance. This materiality is often emphasized by the use of typographic elements and graphic symbols, which are read as a series of visual codes rather than a pictorial image. Graphic design is, therefore, a product with a complex range of signifiers—the visual lexicon of design vocabulary.

Meaning is communicated through the plasticity of materials, the physical nature of the object (such as the weight and size of a book, or the thickness and surface texture of its pages), the printed surface and often the inclusion of photographic images, and the visual codes and languages of typographic detail and composition, color, harmony, balance, and tone. The tactile nature of designed objects that are intended to be held in the hand (such as books, magazines, packaging, or postcards) carries meaning in a similar manner to the surface texture and brushwork of a painting, or the ergonomic nature of a

Practical Considerations

piece of product design, though this element of the design is often overlooked in favor of the printed message and communication contained within.

The signifying nature of materials is important within certain areas of the graphic designer's craft, particularly in the communication of quality or tactility in fields such as book design or packaging. Graphic designers should therefore pay close attention to the materials with which their work is reproduced, particularly where the resulting object is designed to be touched or held in the hand.

> *Sustaining focus and concentration for thirty minutes is one thing, sustaining it for thirty hours or thirty days is something else. And even though time is not in itself a guarantee of excellence it allows for the possibility of contemplation, of refinement, of assessment and reassessment, and of perfecting, in the creation of the things we make, and often on the way they are received and understood. So the temporal signature tells us something about process. In this sense time, or our perception of it, is as significant as any other information we obtain.*
> Andrew Howard, "The Aura of Time," *Design Observer*, December 9, 2014.

At the same time, the denotative meaning of a piece of visual communication is usually contained within the visual forms arranged on its surface: a poster, for instance, which is designed to be viewed from a distance, relies more heavily on the visual composition of graphic elements than on the material on which it is printed to convey its message. Viewed at close proximity, we may be able to observe the texture of the paper, the thickness of the inks, and the composition of color overlays and dot patterns, but such

forensic examination is not the standard function of a poster format, which is usually designed to be read from afar within a public arena. It should also be noted that the ephemeral nature of much graphic design output does go some way to explain the nature of designed artifacts as material objects. Necessity, budget, and the speed of production can play a major role in limiting the range of materials selected to complete a project. The choice of paper for printing long runs of flyers or posters, for instance, is often driven by cost considerations, together with availability and the standard supply networks, account practices, and technical processes of the printing bureau dealing with the production, rather than the tactility, quality, or durability of the material.

Form Follows Technology

Developing technologies also play a major role in the material nature of graphic design artifacts. As print and screen technologies develop, so new working methods and aesthetic possibilities are opened up for the designer. The history of graphic design as a subject is inherently intertwined with that of developing print, mechanical, and, more recently, electronic reproduction processes; from letterpress, lithographic, and digital printing to the evolution of the World Wide Web and interactive digital technologies, with the latter now moving back toward at least a sense of a tactile experience through the development of sophisticated touch-screen interfaces.

Each new technology has seen a shift in contemporary graphic design aesthetics, and design historians have made detailed studies of the impact of each change in both working methods and materials. The development of increasingly sophisticated photolithographic printing techniques between the 1870s and 1950s, for instance, prefigured a widespread shift to the inclusion of

Practical Considerations

photographs—rather than woodcuts, etchings, and hand-drawn illustrations—within a range of inexpensive printed matter, such as posters and magazines. Similarly, the late 1980s and 1990s saw the development of a range of previously inconceivable design methods, which could be achieved only through the use of computer technology. The 21st century witnessed an explosion in the use of peer-to-peer and social networking through the Internet, together with the growth of multifunctional mobile devices for communication, information retrieval, and social networking. Designers have had to adapt quickly to the potentials of these new environments.

The process of materials experimentation runs in parallel to the processes discussed in **Chapter 5: Theory in Practice**, but whereas the visual research methodology is primarily concerned with the composition and arrangement of visual elements, materials research follows similar investigations with the tactile form of the designed object. These two areas go hand in hand, of course: the materials always affect the surface aesthetic as well as adding to the complex chain of signifiers and visual grammar of the object, through which the reader or viewer derives meaning. Senses other than sight may also play a part, communicating through the size, weight, volume, and feel of the designed artifact. Through a range of tests related to the visual and tactile form of the graphic outcome of a project, the designer can help focus the intended message more clearly in the eyes, and hands, of the reader.

The Production Process
Quantitative methods do apply quite strongly, however, in the areas of materials investigation and technology. If a piece of work is to be produced in multiple numbers

(as almost all graphic design is), then the criteria for choice of materials—its resistance to age deterioration or discoloration, distortion, stability, and its fitness for purpose—can be subject to quantitative evaluation. Materials testing (through the use of alternative substrates and surfaces on which to print or technologies to view online data) is an important area of design experimentation, and the results of research within this area can usually be measured with some degree of accuracy.

Similarly, the cost implications involved in the selection of alternative materials and production methods can be compared and measured against the constraints of the project budget. When a piece of work is to be manufactured as a long production run, especially in printed form, the costs involved in even the smallest design decision are magnified accordingly—from the cost of ink and paper to the time and labor involved in folding, collating, cutting, and finishing the final artifact. Printers set up their machines to operate using the most common formats and production runs. This usually implies a reliance on standard International Organization for Standardization (ISO) or imperial paper sizes and color palettes (the CMYK four-color process or Pantone spot colors, for instance). If the designer chooses to work outside of these standards, setup times for production will be longer and the costs will, therefore, increase. As such, the economic aspects and implications of the project need to be planned carefully in advance, and quantitative methods can be useful for the designer in calculating the budget for the project.

1. Edwards, E., and Hart, J. (2004). *Photographs Objects Histories: On the Materiality of Images*. New York: Routledge, 14.

Key Concept: Affordance

The concept of *affordance* was first introduced by the perception theorist James J. Gibson in his book *The Ecological Approach to Visual Perception*, which was first published in 1979. The term has since been used in a variety of fields including cognitive psychology, environmental psychology, industrial design, interaction design, and artificial intelligence, to describe human interaction with objects.

Affordances are the range of possibilities (sometimes termed agency—the ability to act) that an object or environment offers (or appears to offer) to an individual (often termed an actor) in order to perform an action upon it (to do something with that object). Gibson defined affordances as all "action possibilities" latent in the environment relative to the specific actor or audience and their preconceptions of the form, materials, and context of the situation. The affordance of an object or environment then depends not only on the physical capabilities of the actors, but also their goals, beliefs, and past experiences—often described as an individual or collective worldview.

In his groundbreaking 1988 book *The Design of Everyday Things,* Donald A. Norman extended the theory into the realm of product and interaction design. In product design, where one deals with real, physical objects, Norman asserts that there can be both real and perceived affordances, and the two need not be the same. More recently, Norman has further refined the concept to apply to the design of user interfaces and interaction design, noting that "in design, we care much more about what the user perceives than what is actually true. What the designer cares about is whether the user perceives that some action is possible (or in the case of perceived non-affordances, not possible)."[2] Within any form of design,

the designer is hoping to elicit some kind of reaction from the audience or user, and affordance can be thought of as the ways in which the object itself communicates those potential uses or reactions.

The classic example of an affordance in terms of a simple, everyday object is that of the door opener, whereby the presence of a flat metal plate would indicate that the user needs to push, whereas a grab handle would indicate the need to pull the door open. Norman goes on to explain how the reinforced glass panels erected on platforms by a railway company and used as the shelters for passengers were shattered by vandals, and subsequently broken again as soon as they were replaced, in an ongoing cycle of destruction. The situation changed when workmen substituted the glass panels temporarily with plywood boarding, before reinstalling new glass. Although the force needed to break the plywood was equivalent to, or even less than, that of the glass, the shattering stopped. Instead of smashing the boarding, the vandals carved the wood or wrote on its surface. Glass allows us to see through it and can be shattered into a thousand pieces. In this "psychology of materials," the affordances of wood make it rather more appealing to write on or carve than to smash.

2. "Affordances and Design," *Don Norman: Designing for People.* Available online: http://www.jnd.org/dn.mss/affordances_and.html (accessed June 30, 2015).

turn

push

pull

Case Study 10
Public Relations
Designer: Nick Lovegrove

Nick Lovegrove's research project started out as a critical review of the visual language and methods of the public relations (PR) industry, but as he moved through the process, the tone of the work became more disparaging, as indicated by his final research question: *How Can Graphic Design be Used as a Tool to Critique and Expose the Public Relations Industry?* The focus here is on the development of graphic design methods to reveal the hidden structures behind corporate PR messages and the ways in which public announcements are manipulated behind the scenes. Inspired by the critical approach to design outlined in the *First Things First Manifesto* of 1964 and its revised publication in 2000, and with personal experience as a graphic design professional within a television newsroom, Lovegrove had already observed the manner in which PR firms provide a lot of news content and attempt to spin stories to their advantage. As the designer notes, the PR company's "message is relayed to the public by an individual (the journalist) and an organisation (the media outlet) that are widely perceived to be independent. This gives credibility to a message which may otherwise be treated sceptically."

PR companies have a long history of providing news content for broadcast and print media, although their influence has often been shrouded in mystery. However, several recent controversies have drawn more critical attention to the industry, and as a result it is now publicly questioning its own ethics. Its own trade bodies and magazines have been discussing ethical practices, codes of conduct, and, ironically, how to manage the reputation of the industry. Lovegrove began his research by contacting academics studying journalism and media, in order to verify the extent to which current news content was governed by PR channels and influence. He notes:

I contacted Dr Andy Williams, a lecturer from Cardiff University's School of Journalism who supervised the research into the extent of "churnalism" that was commissioned by Nick Davies for the book Flat Earth News. *His study analysed every domestic story featured within* The Times, The Guardian, *the* Independent, *the* Daily Telegraph, *and the* Daily Mail *for evidence of copied content over two weeklong periods in 2007, a total of 2,207 articles. The study found that only 12% of stories could be said to be sourced entirely by the journalist who wrote the story.*

Hidden Agendas

Lovegrove's initial design response was to use data visualization techniques to show these statistics in graphic form, but he felt that the outcome was too neutral and not rhetorical or persuasive enough to offer a clear critique of the subject. Further research led him to expand his reach beyond the role of PR in the media and to look at corporate branding and positioning and the theme of persona management. Although he felt his initial research direction was clear, it ignored large sections of the other activities of PR companies. Media relations is only one field within the industry, with the vast majority of PR activities hidden from public view. He stated:

The more I read about these unseen practices, the more I thought that I was concentrating on too narrow a field of study and that the entire PR industry needed to be exposed. For example, the manipulation of the media using hidden techniques like leaking documents and "off the record" briefings. Techniques like lobbying, the creation of front

Case Study 10
Public Relations
Designer: Nick Lovegrove

groups, subterfuge and the marginalisation of dissenting voices are employed on behalf of a wide range of clients. Some of the worst examples of behaviour committed by PR firms that I read about were commissioned by governments, not corporations.

Lovegrove conducted further research into the "founding father" of PR, Edward Bernays (1891–1995), whose books *Crystallizing Public Opinion* (1923), *Propaganda* (1928), *Public Relations* (1945), and *Engineering of Consent* (1955) became the cornerstone of the modern PR industry. Inspired by the neutral visual aesthetic of corporate relations and media, Lovegrove chose to begin his practical research by developing a new, hybrid typeface derived from an amalgamation of existing standard fonts from desktop publishing; specifically, those used most commonly in press releases. By slightly offsetting and then blending Arial, Tahoma, and Verdana, he created a style that retains a corporate, bland feel but with subtle elements that are inconsistent or ugly when viewed close up. This effect was particularly noticeable on-screen; when printed, at small sizes the lines merge, resulting in unpredictable shapes. Both effects helped to reflect the designer's critical position, connoting distortion, interference, ugliness, and undesired consequences.

He then set himself another self-initiated brief: "Produce a book that uses both words and imagery to expose both the day-to-day practices and the wider implications of the largely-invisible public relations industry. Aimed at a general, public audience, it could be considered as a piece of visual investigative journalism." The new publication was intended to be an accessible, wide-ranging criticism of the whole PR industry, using an introductory text taken from Bernays' original *Propaganda*

book, followed by a critical visual essay focusing on recent major news stories centered on the ethics of PR. These included the rebranding of Bahrain following civil unrest between 2010–2012, when the government of that country employed a range of Western companies to improve its image internationally, and the media response by oil giant BP to the Deepwater Horizon disaster in the Gulf of Mexico, in 2010. BP had used social media photography site Flickr to publicize high-quality photographic images of their clean-up operation in the Gulf, centered on community engagement and the positive outcomes of the process. These contrasted strongly with news media images of the disaster and its hugely negative impact on the local environment. Lovegrove chose to develop a range of graphic editorial pieces focusing on these contradictions.

Graphic methods employed in the research included layering type and images, the contrasting of positive and negative images of contentious news stories, digital distortion, and an ironic approach to word and image combinations, employing relay to extend, or critique, accepted (or controlled) readings. Lovegrove's final outcome included two books, entitled *Bernays' Propaganda* and *Crisis Communication*, although the visual exploration undertaken throughout his research journey and the process of experimentation with a form of rhetorical graphic language can be seen as the core of the project, rather than any final product or summary.

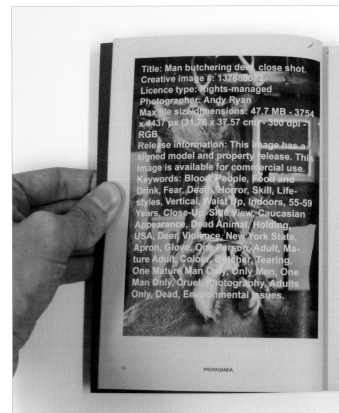

Title: Man butchering deer, close shot.
Creative image #: 137589673
Licence type: Rights-managed
Photographer: Andy Ryan
Max file size/dimensions: 47.7 MB - 3754 x 4437 px (31.78 x 37.57 cm) - 300 dpi - RGB
Release information: This image has a signed model and property release. This image is available for commercial use.
Keywords: Blood, People, Food and Drink, Fear, Death, Horror, Skill, Lifestyles, Vertical, Waist Up, Indoors, 55-59 Years, Close-Up, Side View, Caucasian Appearance, Dead Animal, Holding, USA, Deer, Violence, New York State, Apron, Glove, One Person, Adult, Mature Adult, Colour, Butcher, Tearing, One Mature Man Only, Only Men, One Man Only, Cruel, Photography, Adults Only, Dead, Environmental Issues.

Chapter 1

Organizing Chaos

THE conscious and intelligent manipulation of the organized habits and opinions of the masses is an important element in democratic society. Those who manipulate this unseen mechanism of society constitute an invisible government which is the true ruling power of our country.

We are governed, our minds are molded, our tastes formed, our ideas suggested, largely by men we have never heard of. This is a logical result of the way in which our democratic society is organized. Vast numbers of human beings must cooperate in this manner if they are to live together as a smoothly functioning society. Our invisible governors are, in many cases, unaware of the identity of their fellow members in the inner cabinet.

They govern us by their qualities of natural leadership, their ability to supply needed ideas and by their key position in the social structure. Whatever attitude one chooses to take toward this condition, it remains a fact that in almost every act of our daily lives, whether in the sphere of politics or business, in our social conduct or our ethical thinking, we are dominated by the relatively small number of persons—a trifling fraction of our hundred and twenty million—who understand the mental processes and social patterns of the masses. It is they who pull the wires which control the public mind, who harness old social forces and contrive new ways to bind and guide the world.

It is not usually realized how necessary these invisible governors are to the orderly functioning of our group life. In theory, every citizen may vote for whom he pleases. Our Constitution does not envisage political parties as part of the mechanism of government, and its framers seem not to have pictured to themselves the existence in our national politics of anything like the modern political machine. But the American voters soon found that without organization and direction their individual votes, cast, perhaps, for dozens or hundreds of candidates, would produce nothing but confusion.

Invisible government, in the shape of rudimentary political parties, arose almost overnight.Ever since then we have agreed, for the sake of simplicity and practicality,

M&C Saatchi London $15,226,380

Our presence in the region is dictated by our strategic clients's needs. Hence we follow the lighthouse agency principle consisting of centres of excellence, with extensions into impact point offices where required, allowing ample and timely solutions.

Bell Pottinger London $12,089,645

We tutor clients in what to do when it does break. We help to ensure that the way they react, what they do and, crucially, what others say about them, makes their reputation and doesn't break it.

Case Study 11
CNSRSHP 2.0
Designer: Peter Rüpschl

Peter Rüpschl took a personal interest in the ways that online and social media content is generated and targeted toward individual users in the era of Web 2.0. Entitled *CNSRSHP 2.0: The Invisible Filtering of the Internet*, this research project takes a similarly rhetorical position to Nick Lovegrove's exposure of the PR industry, attempting to reveal the invisible mechanisms at work behind apparently neutral forms of communication. Rüpschl wanted to explore the invisible personalized filtering of Internet content in Web 2.0 and the emerging phenomenon of the "filter bubble." He argues that the filtering of information, targeted at individuals and user groups, is changing the way that we think and behave, isolating us in a narrow bubble of knowledge.

At its heart, some of this filtering process is well-intentioned and valuable to modern society: this might include the protection of people from unsuitable content, such as material of a dangerous, illegal, extremely sensitive, or provocative nature. The Internet is being censored all over the world to prevent citizens from consuming supposedly unsuitable, inappropriate, offensive, and harmful content. The filtering reaches from single words being removed to whole Web sites being filtered out. The range and depth of such control of content varies from country to country. During the uprisings in Egypt in 2011, for instance, the government enforced a nationwide Internet shutdown for a few days in order to suppress people from organizing protests via Facebook and Twitter. Some countries, like China, are even permanently restricting access to a lot of social media sites, and other countries, like Russia, are arresting journalists and bloggers for dissent. Rüpschl argues, however, that such

manipulation of content is not restricted to hardline political regimes, because "in the age of Web 2.0 the internet is getting more and more redesigned in a way that our behavior determines what we get to see."

As the amount of information is growing rapidly, Web sites such as Google and Facebook are responding by integrating more customized algorithmic filters in their services in order to provide the most accurate or appropriate information. Thereby, Web 2.0 is changing the way we read, think, and behave because of the trend of personalizing and tailoring query results on search engines, shortening contextual information on online news sources, and filtering important content on social media sites, based on our interests and likes. This results in an isolated filter bubble, a you-loop of ourselves, filtering out important information that we might not like but that could be crucial for us to know.

Personal Filtering

Facebook is not the only Web site that does this invisible filtering. Google uses 57 signals—depending on who you are, which device you use, and where you are located—to personally filter your search results. Microsoft's search engine Bing even started giving users the option to plug into their Facebook accounts to receive personalized search results based on the opinions of their friends, called Bing Social Search. *The Washington Post* has recently started to provide a personalized news experience based on the user's Facebook profile (called Trove), and more recently, media outlets including *The Huffington Post* are doing the same thing. Search engines, social media sites, and even news sites are becoming "e-butlers," which are filtering relevant information that is personalized for us.

3/10–4/12
UNUSUAL
DOLPHIN
DEATHS
MORE THAN
600
NEW
RECORD
—
7/05–11/06
UNUSUAL
DOLPHIN
DEATHS
190
PREVIOUS
RECORD

A FRIEND'S FIRST SEARCH RESULT ✕ AN OTHER FRIEND'S FIRST SEARCH RESULT

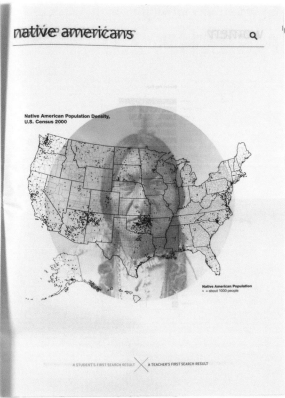

Native American Population Density,
U.S. Census 2000

Native American Population
+ = about 1000 people

A STUDENT'S FIRST SEARCH RESULT ✕ A TEACHER'S FIRST SEARCH RESULT

A TEACHER'S GOOGLE.COM SEARCH RESULTS
A STUDENT'S GOOGLE.COM SEARCH RESULTS THAT ALSO APPEAR IN ◼
A TEACHER'S GOOGLE.COM SEARCH RESULTS THAT DID NOT APPEAR IN ◼

A PUBLIC COMPUTER'S GOOGLE.COM SEARCH RESULTS
A PRIVATE COMPUTER'S GOOGLE.COM SEARCH RESULTS THAT ALSO APPEAR IN ◼
A PUBLIC COMPUTER'S GOOGLE.COM SEARCH RESULTS THAT DID NOT APPEAR IN ◼

Case Study 11
CNSRSHP 2.0
Designer: Peter Rüpschl

Rüpschl notes that:

this tailoring of information has not only transformed the way we think but also the way we read. By permanently reading and writing short text messages on Twitter, Facebook, and via SMS we get used to these short versions of long texts and news. As a result, not only internet services but also traditional media, such as television programs, magazines, and newspapers, adopt to the audience's new expectations by shortening articles and adding text crawls and pop-up ads.

The Daily Me

Today, 36 percent of Americans under age 30 get their daily news from social networking sites, with Facebook being the leading one. Facebook's newsfeed uses algorithmic filters to show information that it believes is most relevant to users, based on their history and interactions. Thereby, the things you like, share, and comment on the most determine what you get to see, whereas postings you don't interact with disappear from your newsfeed. Web 2.0 is changing the way we receive and read information, personalizing and tailoring query results on search engines, shortening contextual information on online news sources, and filtering important content on social media sites based on our interests and likes.

Using various graphic design methods, Rüpschl tried to find a way to reveal the hidden problems that personalized filtering causes. His intention was to raise awareness of the fact that the filter bubble is not just a virtual phenomenon, but that it is a real problem that might change society over the next few generations by altering the way we read,

speak, and behave in everyday communication. After experimenting with the visualization of the consequences of the filter bubble, he decided to shift his focus to three main issues and positions:

- There is no standard Google anymore.
- Popular videos are becoming more relevant than important videos.
- Facebook is becoming people's primary news source.

Rüpschl decided to create three editions of a newspaper-format publication focused on these key themes, using the three screen colors red, green, and blue (RGB), with one color per outcome. His critique of Google personalization techniques drew on information sourced via numerous different Google accounts in response to the same search criteria. For the paper focusing on popular video contents, he interweaved screen stills from popular entertainment and news sources, while the personalized newsfeed paper selected content from a single Facebook profile and reconfigured it into a newspaper format, highlighting the narrow and informal nature of the information.

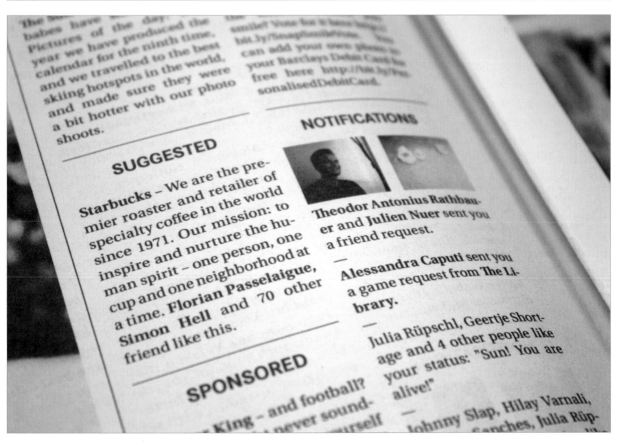

Design Activity 06: Text Messages

Objective

This exercise asks you to consider the role of materials in communicating a message. Donald Norman writes that emotion and cognition work in tandem to create meaning and are both active factors in how we relate to objects. This understanding on the part of the designer can produce interesting solutions to projects based on a range of visceral responses to aspects of design, such as color and materials.

Part 1: Select and Analyze
Select a novel or fictional text and begin to break down the story into several narrative themes contained within the body of the writing. You should use both primary and secondary research methods to develop your analysis, referencing literary theory, historical and cultural contexts, and reader interpretations, together with formal aspects such as grid structure, typographic styles, and page layout.

The text may contain themes underpinning the central narrative that may provide the designer with a context to highlight an alternative iteration of the book. Some stories deal with temporality (e.g., the novel *Dracula* by Bram Stoker), or the descriptive nature of the writing may permit a range of interpretations, such as the references to the sense of smell and aroma in the novel *Perfume* by Patrick Süskind.

Try to think about choosing from a wide range of texts—ones that offer many possible interpretations or readings. The two previous examples are useful case studies, because they have also existed in other media such as film and comic book, and these versions allow us to explore the process of how the printed word has been extended beyond the original authorial position of the writer.

Key Texts

Fawcett-Tang, R. (2005). *Experimental Formats v2: Books, Brochures, Catalogues*. Brighton, England: RotoVision.

Fawcett-Tang, R. (2004). *New Book Design*. London: Laurence King Publishing.

Frascara, J. (1997). *User-Centred Graphic Design*. London: Taylor & Francis.

Hochuli, J. & Kinross, R. (2003). *Designing Books, Practice and Theory*. London: Hyphen Press.

Johnson, B. S. (2007). *The Unfortunates*. New York: New Directions.

Mason, D. & Lewis, A. (2007). *Materials, Process, Print: Creative Solutions for Graphic Design*. London: Laurence King Publishing.

McCaffery, S. & Nichol, B. P. (2000). "The Book as Machine," in *A Book of the Book*. New York: Granary.

McCloud, S. (1994). *Understanding Comics: The Invisible Art*. New York: HarperCollins.

Norman, D. A. (2005). *Emotional Design: Why We Love (or Hate) Everyday Things*. New York: Basic Books.

Perec, G. (2008). *Species of Spaces and Other Pieces*. London: Penguin Classics.

Rawle, G. (2006). *Woman's World: A Graphic Novel*. New York: Atlantic Books.

Safran Foer, J. (2011). *Tree of Codes*. London: Visual Editions.

Smith, K. A. (2003). *The Structure of the Visual Book*. New York: Keith A. Smith Books.

Part 2: Alternative Readings

Start to explore how these other narratives can be revealed within the design of a version of the text. You should attempt to produce a series of iterations that successively build on each other as you develop your ideas and their application.

When addressing projects of this nature, the establishment of the designer's rules of engagement are a vital structure to work within. You might wish to set defined parameters related to the legibility or readability of the text, so that any successful solution may have to address how the text can still be read and understood and that what is added through the design is an augmentation rather than a replacement.

This could involve the use of different paper stocks in order to establish a sense of mood or atmosphere. Color could be used to suggest the passing of time or particular time frames. Typography can be used to extend the meaning of the words or reveal hidden structures within the texts. Perhaps more importantly, a combination of approaches may produce challenging and unlikely outcomes.

A significant aspect of this exercise is the development of a range of alternative iterations that explore a particular aspect or approach, such as how to represent time in a visual manner. In this context, it is better to focus on a smaller aspect of the text—one chapter, or an example section with strong references to the chosen subtext—and to build a range of design outcomes from there. The combination of design approaches employed can then be used to highlight alternative readings of the text.

Sterne, L. (2010). *The Life and Opinions of Tristram Shandy, Gentleman.* London: Visual Editions.

CHAPTER 08
SYNTHESIS

THE INTERRELATIONSHIP BETWEEN THEORETICAL AND PRACTICAL MODELS: APPLICATIONS AND WORKING STRATEGIES FOR THE GRAPHIC DESIGNER WITHIN THE STUDIO ENVIRONMENT

The Process of Synthesis

The concluding stages of any research project involve the convergence of the more successful and effective results of investigations already undertaken in response to the initial problem or idea. The models and methodologies developed at earlier stages can be assessed and built upon as the project develops through a process of iteration and moves toward some form of completion or conclusion.

In their everyday work, designers are continually involved in a process of synthesizing a complex series of factors ranging from technical production processes, budgets, and deadlines to understanding the meanings of messages and addressing intended audiences. The interrelationship of these factors often influences the outcome of a project beyond the designer's original intention. This is not to suggest that this process of synthesis is outside of the designer's control—indeed, a key skill as a designer resides in the ability to prioritize and respond to the various factors emerging in the course of a project.

Research inevitably requires the application of these same skills, but differs slightly in that many of the factors at work will be under the direct control of the designer. The parameters of a brief or research question are often established early on, usually during the investigation of the project's viability through the field of study and the project focus. As a suitable methodology is developed in response to this initial work, these parameters may expand or contract to encompass other aspects, which may in turn influence the methodological approach to the project.

The synthetic aspect of the research process not only builds on the initial stages of the project but also offers the opportunity for critical reflection on the work in general. In projects where the designer has acted in an authorial or self-directed manner, synthesis may also involve reflecting

on the less successful avenues taken in the work, as well as expected and unexpected results.

There is a growing recognition that a wide-ranging education is needed for a synthetic and integrative field such as design to progress. By "synthetic" I mean that design does not have a subject matter of its own— it exists in practice only in relation to the requirements of given projects. Design is integrative in that, by its lack of specific subject matter, it has the potential to connect many disciplines.
Gunnar Swanson, *Graphic Design Education as a Liberal Art* (1994).

Visualizing Research as Subject

In projects where a particular theory or set of theoretical ideas have been explored and tested, the synthesis may require an analysis of how the initial work undertaken can be translated by the designer into a final set of visual outcomes. The questions posed by this kind of research may even result in a set of further questions or proposals as an outcome, encompassing a critical review of potential strategies and methodologies for further development. In this instance, the synthesis of the research may be in the exploration of the most appropriate visual form in which to present the work. This may, for instance, result in work that establishes the context of the question(s) posed or may provide a commentary explaining how the questions were determined.

In applied projects, such as one commissioned by a client or a project rooted in a particular industrial context, the synthesis will entail the analysis of several detailed factors. These would include the historical and contemporary background to the project—taking existing precedents, established conventions, visual or stylistic tropes, and the wider context of the work into account—its audience, and its relationship to other existing work in the area under investigation, as well as an exploration of relevant media, including materials and production processes, projected costs, and possible alternatives. This information will be combined with specific technological and budgetary considerations and a reflection on any testing and feedback that has taken place.

In commercial practice, a survey of potential strategies for development, alongside competitors and restrictions faced, would often take the form of a Strengths, Weaknesses, Opportunities, and Threats (SWOT) analysis and a Political, Economic, Social, and Technological (PEST) analysis—a common approach in the fields of marketing and advertising, which may in some cases have a similar relevance to design methodologies. This critique of the research question and the contextual framework provides the basis for the final stages of the research, which will converge this information into an outcome or solution. Derived from market research and economics, SWOT and PEST are two systems of analysis linked to the development of proposals or strategies and their predicted outcomes.

SWOT analysis describes an examination of the *internal* Strengths and Weaknesses and *external* Opportunities and Threats affecting an organization or design proposal; it is used to make projections for the proposed research activities. Typically, the analysis seeks to answer two general questions: (1) What is the current status of the proposed problem or question? and (2) What is the intention or goal of the proposal? PEST analysis describes a strategic review of the Political, Economic, Social, and Technological factors that may

impact on the proposed project. It is a part of the *external* analysis when conducting a strategic review or doing market research, and it gives an overview of the different macroenvironmental factors that the designer has to consider. It is a useful strategic tool for understanding the market and audience, business potential, cost and technological implications, and direction for operations.

In some cases, the methodology employed may be the outcome to the project in itself, rather than a developmental phase. This can take several forms, including the documentation of individual but related tests, which chart the progress of the investigation. This is particularly relevant in areas such as materials testing, or in those projects that survey a subject area but do not attempt to reach a specific designed outcome or resolution. Projects in this area would include Orlagh O'Brien's investigation into the mapping of emotions (pages 100-107), Nick Lovegrove's visual exploration of the conventions and tools utilized within the public relations industry (pages 174-179), and Paul McNeil's deconstruction of type and letterforms (pages 204-211), all of which present designed summaries of the exploration undertaken, together with a critical reflection on the body of knowledge gained from that research, rather than attempting to define a particular problem or need.

As with any valid research question, the outcome of a project is not immediately predictable: if it were, there would be no need to undertake the research. It is therefore important to develop a degree of flexibility within a working research methodology. During the final stages of a research project, early ideas can often be transformed to suggest several unexpected or alternative outcomes. It could be argued that this flexibility is inherent in graphic

The Process of Synthesis

design practice, and that it is part of the intuitive approach of many designers.

> *It is necessary for designers to recognize the needs of the social and physical environment within which they work and to which they contribute, and to take conscious steps to define the future direction of their profession. For this to happen, designers will have to develop new tools, engage in interdisciplinary teams, initiate projects, generate new information and share it.*
>
> Jorge Frascara, *User-centred Graphic Design: Mass Communications and Social Change* (1997).

The Designer's Voice

Within the field of design authorship (see pages 042-043), particularly research utilizing graphic design systems and methods in the interrogation of a subject of interest to the designer—research through design—the critical position or voice of the author is an important aspect for consideration. Relating closely to the designer's intentions, the design voice refers to the way in which the project is intended to be perceived by its audience: that voice could be critical, political, ironic, humorous, informative, or educational, for instance. It may be transparent to a degree—in the typographic composition of a book or in many forms of information design—but it is never neutral. As a mediator and facilitator of communication, the designer occupies a unique position, and the axis between pure translation of a client's brief and subjective intervention in the actual form and content of the message is at the heart of the debate concerning the social and political position of design as an engaged form of practice.

The notion of critical thinking as a tradition within Western academic discourse has been developed by educational theorist Professor Ronald Barnett in his 1997 book *Higher Education: A Critical Business*. Barnett argues that a perceived limitation of critical thinking is inherent in its contextualization within the academic environment, rather than as a part of an approach to life in general. He goes on to describe an alternative notion of "critical being," extended from the concept of critical thinking and defined as an approach to life that includes thinking, self-reflection, and action: "Critical persons are more than just critical thinkers. They are able critically to engage with the world and with themselves as well as with knowledge." In this sense, critical being is an approach to life, thinking, and criticality that university-educated people should aspire to, taking their questioning and rational mind beyond the walls of the university and out into the wider world.

This sense of critical being would seem essential to a socially and culturally engaged graphic design practice. Design both reflects and shapes wider cultural concerns, conventions, and stereotypes. Where such conventions are subject to criticism, design has an important role to play in facilitating progressive change. An informed or engaged practitioner in graphic design may well be operating from a distinct personal position with many central concerns in their work that extend beyond individual projects. Engaged practice may be driven by social, political, moral, or other ideological positions about the function and consequences of design production. Debate about this area of working has informed the discourse surrounding the discipline of graphic design in recent years and could be seen as part of the discussion surrounding the notion of graphic design and authorship.

The Process of Synthesis

Creative Solutions

The Dutch graphic designer Jan van Toorn has described the designer as a "practical intellectual . . . someone who is actively engaged in critical reflection about the designer's process of making."[1] It is this activity of "critical reflection" that van Toorn suggests is crucial to the designer's research. In fact, van Toorn relates the notion of the practical intellectual to an informed and engaged practice in general. This approach to graphic design is rooted both in the practice and a reflection on that practice and is closer to the more accepted notion of graphic design (at least from within the discipline) as a problem-solving activity.

Meanwhile, the American writer, designer, and educator Andrew Blauvelt argues for a closer integration of theory and practice and a critical reflection in work, rather than about work:

> [C]ritical thinking and making skills are crucial for success. . . . Questions that cannot be answered with a simple yes or no are, in fact, research questions. And if the practice of graphic design is more than an unending series of solutions to never-ending problems, then we might begin to understand graphic design as a researchable activity, subject to both the limits of theory and the limitations of practice.[2]

Graphic design research then includes the range of methodologies employed in the planning and development of practical work, together with the critical evaluation of both that process and the work itself.

The methods outlined in this book are an attempt to move beyond the already overstated case for intuition and the designer's creativity and imagination. When the subject of creativity is introduced in design debate, it often masks a laziness on the part of its advocates—an unwillingness to engage in a more rigorous and exacting procedure for making, and a fear that, if revealed, it might alienate clients and audience alike. Far from adding what has been described as "intellectual glamor" to the practice of graphic design, the adherence and commitment to a method of working, grounded in research and practical methods with clear aims, is a significant development in the growth of the discipline.

Cultural Signs

A text might be an image, object, artifact or place that can be read, allowing for historical, cultural, or social interpretation. The El Morro National Monument is located on an ancient east–west trail in western New Mexico. Carvings were originally made at the site by the Anasazi Indians, and these were added to by further settlers from Spain and Mexico during the 17th and 18th centuries. As a key watering hole in the western desert, the site became hugely important to US settlers heading west during the 19th century, and many of them carved signatures, names, and dates into the rock.

1. van Toorn, J. "Thinking the Visual: Essayistic Fragments on Communicative Action," in Bouman, O. (ed.). (1994). "And Justice for all . . .", Maastricht: Jan van Eyck Akademie Editions, pp. 140-152.
2. Blauvelt, A. "Remaking Theory, Rethinking Practice," in Heller, S. (1997). The Education of a Graphic Designer, New York: Allworth Press, p. 102.

Key Concept: Rubbish Theory

First proposed by Michael Thompson in his book of the same name (1979), *Rubbish Theory* relates to the creation and destruction of value within manmade objects, cultural artifacts, and even ideas. As a social scientist, Thompson became interested in the ways in which objects carry an economic or cultural value, which diminishes over time, to the point where they become redundant and worthless. However, Thompson noted that some objects then begin to accrue value once more as time goes on, such as antiques, vintage cars, and Georgian terraced houses.

Objects can then make the journey from a region Thompson describes as *transient* (value decreasing), through *rubbish* (no value), to *durable* (value increasing). When this idea is applied to a house, for example, we can see that a building may have an initially high value, dependent on status, cost, and function, which may decrease over time in relation to an expected lifespan, after which it may have little or no residual value and could be demolished to make way for a new building in its place. However, although this obsolescence tends to happen with certain kinds of property (low-cost housing built in the 1960s, for example), it is not the case with Georgian or Victorian English townhouses, which the real estate agent terms "period properties" and which are then considered highly desirable and expensive. The notion of durability is, thus, socially constructed.

The actions of an individual relate to his or her own worldview—the way in which he or she perceives the world, based on cultural heritage, education, and experience. Thompson's theory attempts to draw our attention to the ways in which our understanding of objects is socially constructed and understood. He goes further in refuting the ideals of transaction theory, whereby an agreement is implied between individuals transacting over a valued object, based on their range of shared assumptions.

Although different, these assumptions are harmonized over time because of each individual adapting his or her approach and worldview in order to achieve better results in the next transaction, which leads to the homogeneous worldview (or shared cultural values) of a social group or community. Thompson argues that this process is, by definition, static in its exclusion of the range of external influences on the individuals involved, and the fact that their perception of the results of their actions may be different from reality. These ideas are useful to the producers of transient and durable objects—such as graphic designers—in helping to describe the complex relationship between the cultural artifact and its perceived value or use.

Case Study 12
Hauntology and Urban Planning
Designer: Rob Mowbray

Sometimes the driver for a self-authored research project arises from the designer's interest in the theory itself. This was true in Rob Mowbray's case, with the principal aim of this project being a thorough, practice-based investigation into the philosophical concept of hauntology. His intention from the outset was to demonstrate how such a theoretical framework might be employed by the graphic designer in order to visually communicate the key hauntological components of trace, dyschronia, and mourning. By combining this investigation with a psychogeographical interpretation of the urban environment, the objective was to produce an outcome that functions as a visual critique of the contemporary sociopolitical landscape.

Seeking a practical vehicle for the work and a set of theoretical boundaries to work within, Mowbray chose to articulate these concepts using the London Borough of Croydon as a case study, to illustrate the consequences of the borough's town planning decisions of the 1960s, while reasserting the power of graphic design as a catalyst for change. For the past twenty-five years, many graphic designers have generally been happy to define their output as postmodern. Mowbray's critique asserts that this wholehearted embrace of so-called low popular culture is a desperate attempt to remain at the shallow end of the popular arts:

Where design was once a sign of ideology, consumer culture has rendered it as mere style and personal aesthetic expression. Radical style and commercial style become instantly inseparable. Design that was once deemed revolutionary now looks like standard commercial culture in the dazzling spectacle of infotainment.

Croydon is a borough of South London experiencing a crisis of identity. The largest populated of the London boroughs, it was incorporated into Greater London in 1965. Having been comprehensively bombed during the war, it was widely redeveloped afterward. The local council has made repeated failed attempts to achieve city status, with successive councils attempting to build a new "vision for Croydon," but the locality has been unable to divest itself of a reputation forged by the highly questionable town planning decisions of the 1960s. Between 1956 and 1972, nearly six million square feet of office space, a major shopping center, and an ill-conceived ring road were built in the town's center, largely at the expense of Victorian housing, public halls, and school playing fields. The scale of this redevelopment is responsible for Croydon's current reputation as a bleak, characterless, concrete jungle. Mowbray relates this to his theoretical premise: "In hauntological terms, the ghosts of 20th century town planning continue to haunt the splintered rationalization of this dystopian non-place."

Before the arrival of the town's skyscrapers, the Town Hall clock tower, built in 1896, was the tallest building in Croydon. The 1950s witnessed a new fascination with anything that reached into the heavens. The Apollo House and Lunar House office blocks in Croydon were named in homage to a new era of space-age utopianism. By 1972 there were fifty-six office blocks of more than 1,000 square feet in the Croydon town center. Twenty-nine of these blocks were over ten stories tall and were the head offices for a host of large companies, including Nestlé, RAC, Tate & Lyle, Brooke Bond-Oxo, Lennig Chemicals, IBM, Black Clawson, Roneo, and Rothschild's, as well as a collection of insurance companies, financial services and construction industry firms, government departments, and nationalized industries. The town center provided employment for more than 20,000 workers: Croydon had rapidly become

CORINTHIAN HOUSE, CROYDON

N.L.A. TOWER, CROYDON · T.04456.01

Norfolk House, Croydon

Rothschild House, Whitgift Centre

Suffolk House, George Street

Case Study 12
Hauntology and Urban Planning
Designer: Rob Mowbray

one of the largest centers of office growth in the country, outside of central London.

Croydon's latest metamorphosis, Croydon Vision 2020, is a regeneration program that seeks to promote the town as "a hub of living, retailing, culture and business in South East England." Plans include the construction of yet more office space, residential tower blocks, and the creation of a sprawling shopping center.

Mowbray gathered historical data on Croydon from the Local History Study Archive at Croydon Central Library, ranging from newspaper articles and photographs to 1970s planning maps. He was also able to trace the various names the individual buildings have been known by, as well as the names of their architects and developers. He chose to focus the research on the office blocks that were developed as a direct result of the Croydon Corporation Act, particularly those that have since been demolished or redeveloped.

An early design concept involved the creation of a series of glyphs depicting the visual language of Croydon, based on observational photographs from wandering the town center. This was followed by the creation of a newspaper inspired by the *Suburban Press* agitprop magazine that had been produced by artist/designer Jamie Reid in the same area in the early 1970s. In this publication, Mowbray employed several graphic techniques intended to evoke a historical resonance. Photographs were manipulated to emulate the type of oversaturation reminiscent of 1960s postcard imagery, while a combination of torn paper clippings, collage, and period typefaces emulate the lo-fi, détourned aesthetic of the original *Suburban Press*. Key phrases in the newspaper were drawn from the language of Croydon's commercial real estate agents, as Mowbray asserts: "These manifestos

of hyperreality typically contain over enthusiastic phrases such as: 'strategic framework,' 'social infrastructure,' 'growth potential,' 'vertically integrated,' 'return on equity,' 'premium outlet' and 'exciting retail destination.'"

From the outset, Mowbray was keen to utilize concrete as a medium to communicate what he saw as Croydon's architectural malaise and to offer a visual critique of the totalizing dogma of town planning—the manner in which the "spectre of the past haunts the contemporary urban environment." The urban architectural scale model is the ubiquitous tool of the urban planner, giving architects the perspective of those who view the city from above—the god view. Mowbray decided to construct forty-three cement maquettes representing each of the remaining office buildings (of more than 1,000 square feet) constructed in Croydon between 1956 and 1972. The scale of each maquette was determined by the height and total floorspace of the original building, and each one was laser engraved with an image of the appropriate building. The final collected work, entitled *Sir James Marshall Psychogeographic Memorial: The Hauntological Convergence of Private Enterprise, Urban Planning and Ghosts ... in Croydon*, was presented in a large, gridded wooden box, with the maquettes sitting inside dedicated spaces, surrounding a single copy of the agitprop newspaper and overlaid with a Perspex sheet silkscreen printed with a range of individual glyphs from his first experiment to visualize the identity of the town. The object is deliberately monumental in scale and weight—a reflection on its content and the sense of the past overlaying the present, from which the area can never seem to escape.

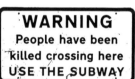

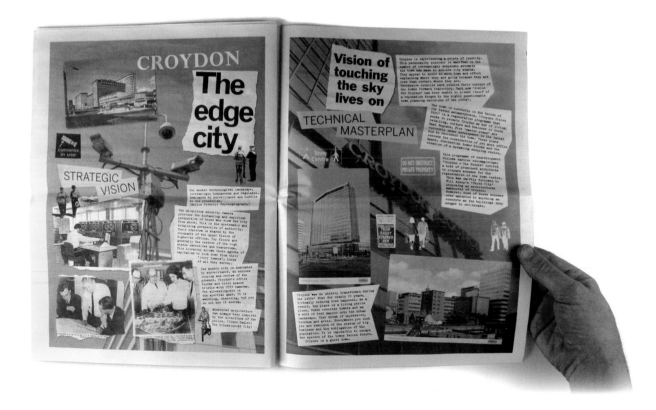

Case Study 13
Language and Text
Designer: Paul McNeil

Originally published in the first edition of *Visual Research* in 2005, graphic designer Paul McNeil's structured series of investigations into type, text, and language are centered on a reiterative series of visual experiments. McNeil's interest in writing systems and his background in professional design practice provided much of the original impetus for the project. He established a systematic way of working that allowed him to undertake a wide variety of tightly focused experiments, each of which attempted to address individual aspects of the overall objective of the work: to define—or, at least, describe—a set of possible systemic parameters for the formulation of the visible word. By electing to work within a common visual framework for each aspect of the project, using a consistent range of possible print formats, he was able to make a comparative analysis of the work as it progressed. Although each subproject can be viewed independently, as a stand-alone investigation, the intention was to use each experimental stage to inform the next stage and to build progressively toward a collection of volumes that, in themselves, would make up the final outcome to the project. McNeil describes these individual elements as "topographic fragments of a work in progress."

Each of these subprojects was produced in a standard format comprising a proposition, a methodology, and a series of subsequent visual tests. By purposefully controlling the scope of each project, McNeil was able to "do a lot with a little," interrogating particular aspects of written language in detail. This allowed him to be continuously aware of his decision-making processes and to build on them as a significant aspect of his approach, while also allowing for digression and failure. Individual experiments explored different aspects of typographic form and language. These ranged from simple investigations, such as the effects of

symmetry on letters of the Roman alphabet, to the creation of visual systems generated by the frequency of letters and sounds in speech. Experiments with mirroring examined aspects of symmetry and asymmetry in the Roman alphabet in order to uncover hidden forms and possible suggestions of lost images within individual glyphs. Having classified letterforms by symmetrical type (conforming to a vertical axis, horizontal axis, angled axis, double axis, rotational axis, or asymmetrical axis), basic symmetries were recorded photographically, using mirrors placed over gridded outputs of the characters. In another experiment, a unicase alphabet attempts to reduce the inherent ambiguity and redundancy of the Roman alphabet by amalgamating variant uppercase and lowercase glyphs from a total of forty-two to twenty-six—the higher number being accountable to the visual differences between characters such as E/e, A/a, and R/r. The intention was to increase legibility by maximizing key differences between glyphs.

This process of critical making builds on Jan van Toorn's concept of the graphic designer as the "practical intellectual," an individual who is engaged in critical reflection about the designer's process of making. McNeil has made this notion a central feature of his work, advancing the idea by focusing on how it is documented and communicated. He describes the overall objective of the project as "dedicated not solely towards its subject—writing and language systems—but to transferable parametric methods, to algorithmic systems in general, and to a conscious personal rediscovery of the pleasures of visual research." In each case, McNeil developed a methodology that allowed him to document his exploration of a particular theme, such as tonal frequency, but also to find an appropriate manner to convey the ideas so that they could provide a concurrent visual commentary on the work as it progressed.

In a final series of visual experiments, McNeil employed a range of approaches adopted from the field of generative design in the process of form making. The phrase—drawn from related subjects such as architecture, computing, and engineering—is intended to encompass design activities that have a direct influence on the form of what is produced. The study or use of generative systems as part of a working design research methodology involves an understanding of the explicit relationship between the systematic (the process, considerations, and decision-making processes) and the final visual form or product (its properties, composition, and performance). In the case of Paul McNeil's work, this involved the development of a series of tests that eventually led to the creation of a visual system that would automatically generate printed forms—in this case, letterforms based on sets of components and conditions. By defining the range of individual component parts of the alphabet—the strokes and dots that make letters—McNeil could devise systems to generate all of the possible typographic forms that could be constructed from them. The hierarchy of stroke types in the alphabet was classified into separate components and then reconstructed using every combination of stroke type.

Characters were categorized by the lines used: curvilinear, elliptical, and circular strokes, vertical strokes, horizontal strokes, and diagonal strokes. Following the research conducted into individual letterforms and their frequency of use in the English language, McNeil extended his range of experiments to look at the internal typographic structure of letterforms and their use within an alphabetic system of differences. To playfully examine the significance of internal glyph skeletons in conveying meaning, he constructed a typeface that is capable of generating words and sentences, but that disallows the appearance of individual letterforms. Internal character shapes are forced to merge, leaving only the exoskeletons of word forms, although traditional typographic patterns are retained so that, at first glance, texts look correct.

Critical Reflections:—An Interview with the Designer

Paul McNeil began his academic career on graduating from the masters course in 2005 and since 2008 has worked as a full-time lecturer in the postgraduate area at London College of Communication, running an MA in typography. He is a partner in MuirMcNeil, a collaboration with fellow designer Hamish Muir, set up in 2010 to explore parametric design methods. They work on their own joint projects and on professional briefs. In addition, he is currently researching and writing an extensive history of typography.

How has your subsequent career developed?
Before undertaking my academic studies, I'd worked in design practice for many years. At that time, I was keen to reorient my career to find a sustainable balance between the kind of self-initiated work one can undertake in education and commissioned projects. A decade ago, I was solely committed to fulfilling client briefs. Today, I'm involved in lots of different things and working with lots of different people. Is the grass greener? Absolutely.

How do you now feel about the methods developed within this project? Have you applied them any further in your own personal practice or professional work?
The course I undertook placed methods in the foreground, and to some extent my project work was (and is) an exercise deliberately intended to investigate them: to make method a subject rather than a project. I took the opportunity to consciously reflect on the ways in

Case Study 13
Language and Text
Designer: Paul McNeil

which decision-based processes and interactions give rise to communicative forms. Having spent much of my life literally identified (whether accurately or not) as a "creative," it was hugely beneficial to me to work openly with the specifics of design processes, to explore alternative approaches to making, and to discover generative design. I continue to find ideas about generativity highly compelling and very liberating. My recent MuirMcNeil projects illustrate this (see pages 212–213). We ask very specific, limited questions about aspects of form, set up conditions for exploring them, and then execute as many possible visual investigations as we can within the limits of time, money, and our abilities. Our designs—typefaces and posters—are simply records of our investigations, waypoints on a hugely enjoyable journey. This precisely replicates what I came to understand through study.

What other elements do you feel could or should be considered when undertaking a similar project—on reflection, how would you change or refine the process?
I might answer this by saying that I wish I had found a clearer question at the outset. But that doesn't really matter to me. What counts is the will, the desire to discover, to learn, and hopefully to understand. My question still isn't clear—that's why I'm still working on it.

Crucially, also, I think that too much emphasis is placed on having big ideas nowadays. I see students struggle all the time to find them in the wrong place— within themselves—rather than through hard work involving conjecture, knowledge acquisition, skills training, exploration, observation, evaluation, etc. In such a framework, the method and the subject of inquiry begin to achieve equanimity. Thinking of methods as mere routes toward solutions is as erroneous and wasteful as divorcing

songs from singing. A graphic designer is nothing at all if not a form-giver, and what makes a "designerly way of knowing" uniquely valuable is that it can only ever be achieved through making, seeing, and seeking to improve. This idea was best put by Steve Jobs in an interview:

You know, one of the things that really hurt Apple was after I left John Sculley got a very serious disease. It's the disease of thinking that a really great idea is 90% of the work. And if you just tell all these other people "here's this great idea," then of course they can go off and make it happen.

And the problem with that is that there's just a tremendous amount of craftsmanship in between a great idea and a great product. And as you evolve that great idea, it changes and grows. It never comes out like it starts because you learn a lot more as you get into the subtleties of it. And you also find there are tremendous tradeoffs that you have to make. There are just certain things you can't make electrons do. There are certain things you can't make plastic do. Or glass do. Or factories do. Or robots do.

Designing a product is keeping five thousand things in your brain and fitting them all together in new and different ways to get what you want. And every day you discover something new that is a new problem or a new opportunity to fit these things together a little differently.

And it's that process that is the magic.[3]

---

3. *Triumph of the Nerds* (2006) [TV program] PBS, June 12 (Steve Jobs interviewed by Robert X. Cringely).

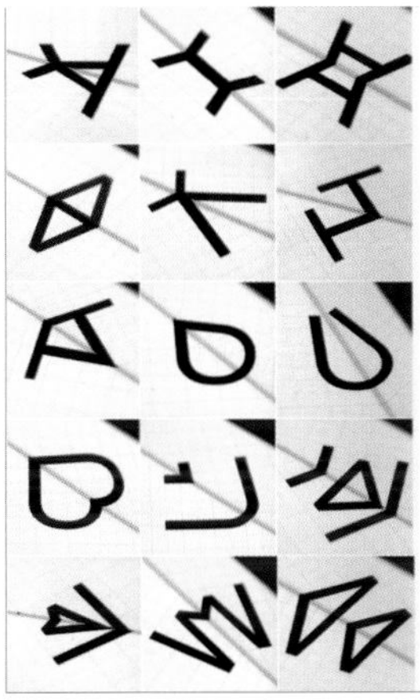

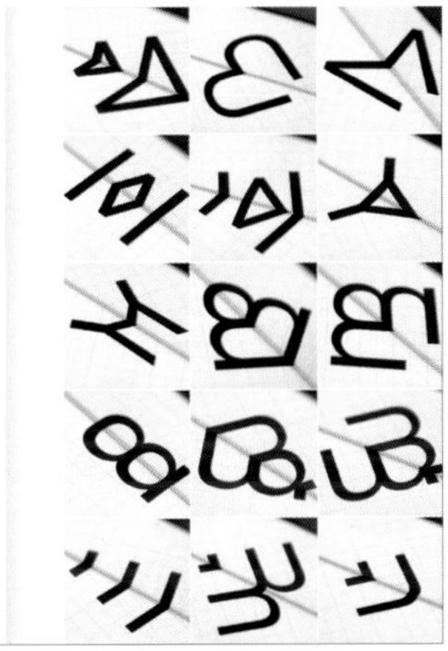

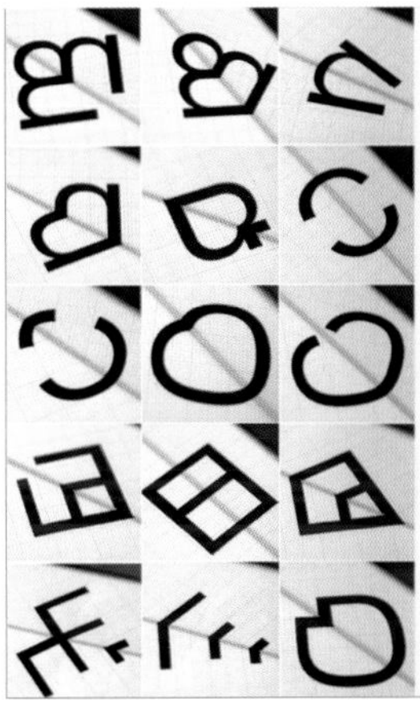

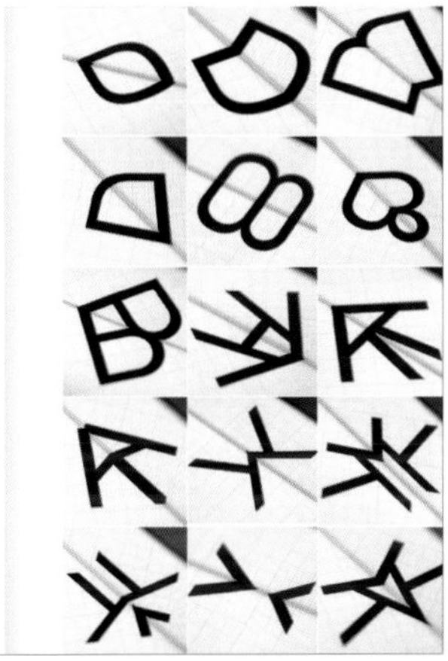

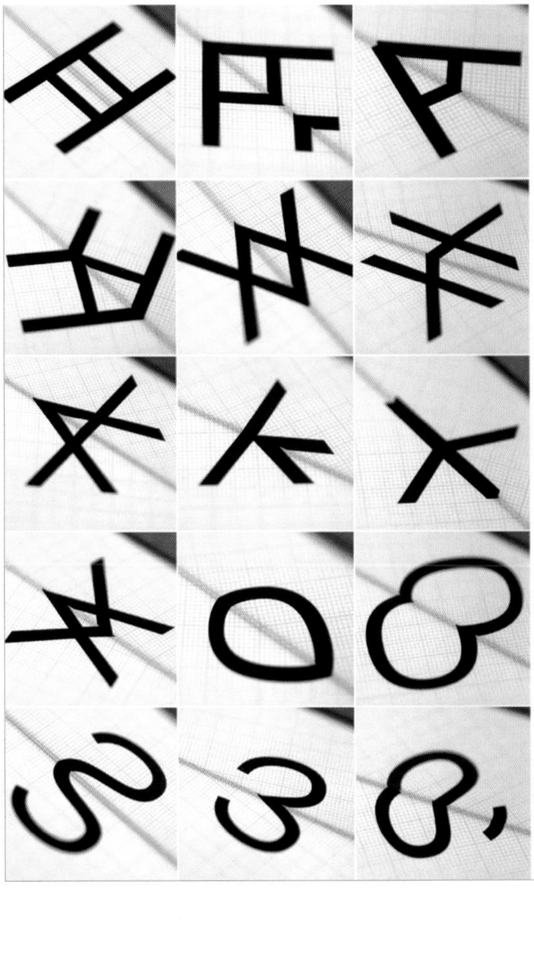

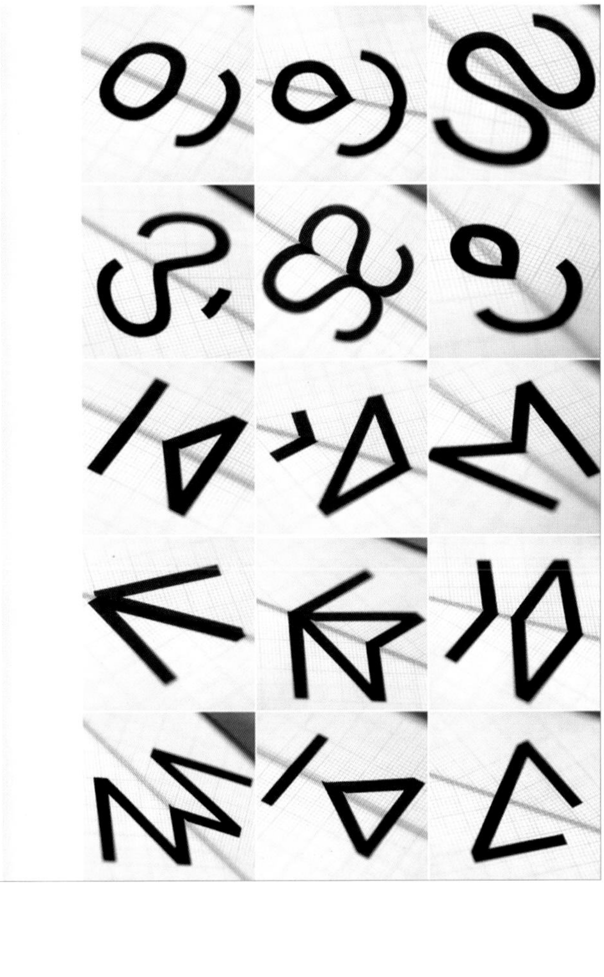

slice
one
two
three
four
five

ABCDEFGHIJKLMNOPQRSTUVWXYZ
abcdefghijklmnopqrstuvwxyz
0123456789

living in the midst of signs
had very slowly brought us to
see as so many signs the
innumerable things that had
at first been there without
indicating anything but their
own presence, it had
transformed them into signs
of themselves, and had
added them to the series of
signs deliberately made by
whoever wanted to make a
sign. the series of signs
multiplied itself into the
series of signs of signs, of
signs repeated an
innumerable number of
times, always the same and
always in some way different
for to the sign made on
purpose was added the sign
fallen there by chance

slice
one
two
three
four
five

ABCDEFGHIJKLMNOPQRSTUVWXYZ
abcdefghijklmnopqrstuvwxyz
0123456789

living in the midst of signs
had very slowly brought us to
see as so many signs the
innumerable things that had
at first been there without
indicating anything but their
own presence, it had
transformed them into signs
of themselves, and had
added them to the series of
signs deliberately made by
whoever wanted to make a
sign. the series of signs
multiplied itself into the
series of signs of signs, of
signs repeated an
innumerable number of
times, always the same and
always in some way different,
for to the sign made on
purpose was added the sign
fallen there by chance

209

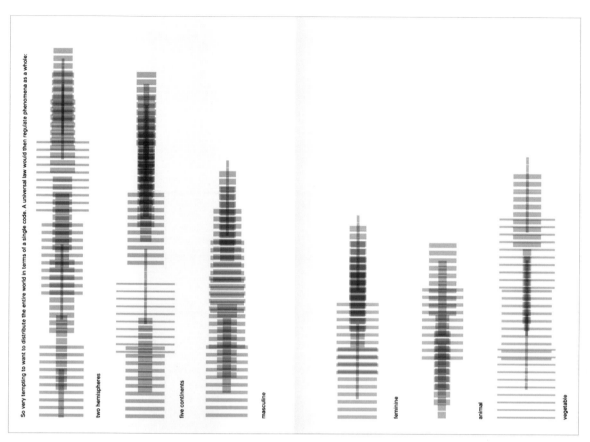

So very tempting to want to distribute the entire world in terms of a single code. A universal law would then regulate phenomena as a whole:

two hemispheres

five continents

masculine

feminine

animal

vegetable

SO VERY TEMPTING TO WANT TO DISTRIBUTE THE ENTIRE WORLD IN TERMS OF A SINGLE CODE. A UNIVERSAL LAW WOULD THEN REGULATE PHENOMENA AS A WHOLE:

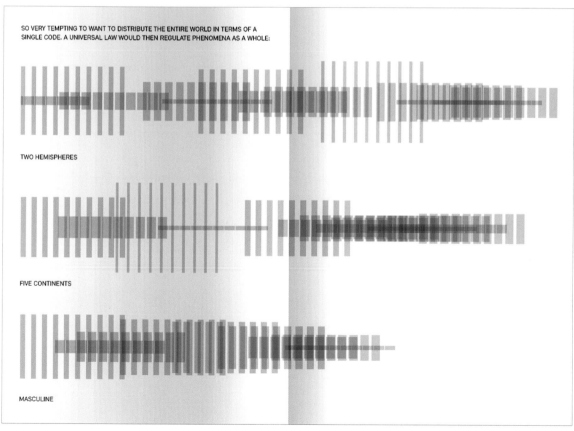

TWO HEMISPHERES

FIVE CONTINENTS

MASCULINE

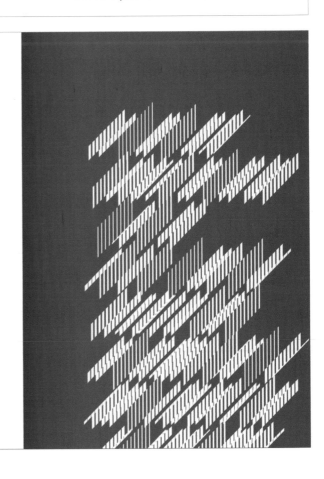

211

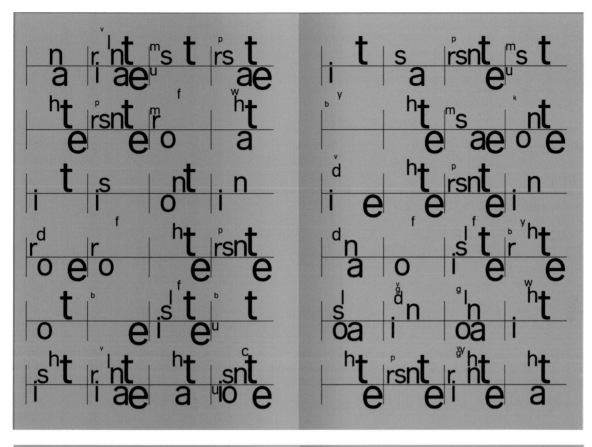

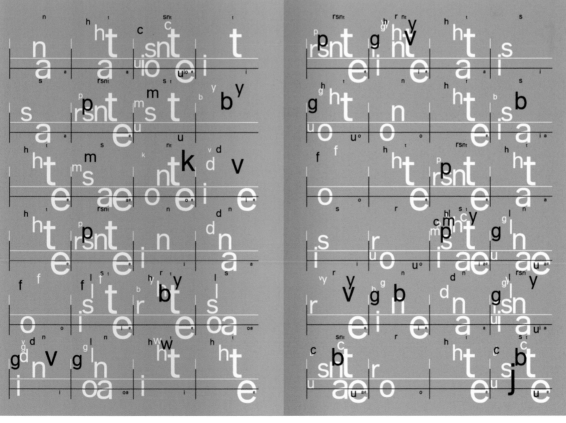

Design Activity 07: Practical Methods

Objective

The aim of this exercise is to enable you to construct a self-initiated project. Designers often look to develop work outside of their day jobs, exploring ideas about design and their own practice that do not necessarily fit within specific commercial briefs and that provide opportunities to investigate a wider range of ideas that will contribute to their ongoing development as designers. Many design courses include a degree of self-initiated work, and often this is a focus for final examination.

When considering how to construct a self-initiated brief, you should begin by thinking about personal areas of interest: things you are excited about or concerns you may have, for example—in short, issues you are passionate about. However, the project should be related to graphic design in either its subject or working methodology (or both). Initial thinking about project topics should reflect your knowledge, critical position, and interests, and should be seen as opportunities to use the expertise, understanding, and skills you have acquired to date.

The following questions will allow you to structure your project and should be considered as the foundations of a successful approach:

Why?
• Has the research question been stated?
• Have project objectives been defined in relation to your broad intentions?

What?
• What specific questions will the project seek to ask?
• Is the focus of the project clearly described?
• Has the context of the project been clearly described?

How?
• Is the methodology clear and understandable?
• Is the project adequately defined in terms of its primary research? (e.g., data gathering, formulation of design concepts and messages, critical reflection and evaluation, consideration of audience, selection of appropriate media/formats, articulation of visual language, media testing)

Key Texts

Barnett, R. (1997), *Higher Education: A Critical Business*. London: Open University Press.

Barthes, R. (1993). *Image Music Text*. London: Fontana Books.

Baxandall, M. (1987). *Patterns of Intention: On the Historical Explanation of Pictures*. New Haven, CT: Yale University Press.

Berger, J. (2008). *Ways of Seeing*. London: Penguin Classics.

Crow, D. (2010). *Visible Signs: An Introduction to Semiotics*, 2nd edition. Worthing, UK: AVA Publishing SA.

Emmison, M., & Smith, P. (2000). *Researching the Visual: Introducing Qualitative Methods*. London: SAGE.

Frascara, J. (1997). *User-Centred Graphic Design*. London: Taylor & Francis.

Harvey, C. (1995). *Databases in Historical Research: Theory, Methods and Applications*. London: Palgrave Macmillan.

Laurel, B. (Ed.). (2004). *Design Research: Methods and Perceptions*. Cambridge, MA: MIT Press.

Lupton, L., & Abbott Miller, J. (1999). *Design, Writing, Research: Writing on Graphic Design*. London: Phaidon Books.

Norman, D. A. (2002). *The Design of Everyday Things*. New York: Basic Books.

O'Sullivan, T., Hartley, J., Saunders, D., Montgomery, M., & Fiske, J. (1994). *Key Concepts in Communication and Cultural Studies*. London: Routledge.

Poynor, R. (2002). *Design Without Boundaries: Visual Communication in Transition*. London: Booth-Clibborn.

Design activity #7

• Is the project adequately defined in terms of its secondary research? (e.g., an interrogation of the field of study, analysis of reference materials, examination of alternative approaches and existing work within the field, relation to wider cultural contexts)

Who?
• Has a potential audience been identified?
• Is the audience significant to the project, and if so, in what way?

When?
• Does the methodology identify clear stages of development?
• Has a detailed work plan/timetable been prepared?

Where?
• Are the general research reference materials relevant, detailed, accurate, and appropriate?

Research documentation is an integral part of the project. A designed and edited visual summary recording all research processes, critically analyzing their methodologies, and seeking to locate the work in its cultural context will form the major part of the project. In some cases, the process of investigation will be the project, and in others the research and testing of ideas will lead to a definitive outcome or artifact.

Poynor, R. (2003). *No More Rules: Graphic Design and Postmodernism.* London: Laurence King.

Poynor, R. (2007). *Obey the Giant: Life in the Image World,* 2nd edition. Basel, Switzerland: Birkhäuser Verlag.

Rose, G. (2006). *Visual Methodologies: An Introduction to the Interpretation of Visual Material.* London: SAGE.

Schön, D. (1984). *The Reflective Practitioner: How Professionals Think in Action.* New York: Basic Books.

Tufte, E. (1997). *Visual and Statistical Thinking: Displays of Evidence for Decision Making.* New York: Graphics Press.

Wolff, J. (1993). *The Social Production of Art.* London: Palgrave Macmillan.

APPENDICES
FURTHER READING, CONTRIBUTING DESIGNERS, INDEX, ACKNOWLEDGMENTS

Further Reading

Armstrong, H. (2009). *Graphic Design Theory: Readings from the Field*. New York: Princeton Architectural Press.

Beirut, M., Drenttel, W., & Heller, S. (1994). *Critical Writings On Graphic Design, Volumes 1, 2, 3*. New York: Allworth Press.

Bennett, A. (2006). *Design Studies: Theory and Research in Graphic Design*. New York: Princeton Architectural Press.

Buchanan, R., & Margolin, V. (Eds.). (1995). *Discovering Design: Explorations in Design Studies*. Chicago: University of Chicago Press.

Cross, N. (2007). *Designerly Ways of Knowing*. Basel, Switzerland: Birkhäuser Verlag.

Crow, D. (2016). *Visible Signs: An Introduction to Semiotics in the Visual Arts*, 3rd edition. London: Bloomsbury.

Emmison, M., & Smith, P. (2000). *Researching the Visual: Introducing Qualitative Methods*. London: SAGE.

Erlhoff, M., & Marshall, T. (Eds.). (2008). *Design Dictionary: Perspectives on Design Terminology*. Basel, Switzerland: Birkhäuser Verlag.

Heller, S., & Finamore, M. E. (Eds.). (1997). *Design Culture: An Anthology of Writing from the AIGA Journal of Graphic Design*. New York: Allworth Press.

Heller, S., & Pomeroy, K. (1997). *Design Literacy: Understanding Graphic Design*. New York: Allworth Press.

Laurel, B. (Ed.). (2003). *Design Research: Methods and Perceptions*. Cambridge, MA: MIT Press.

Leborg, C. (2007). *Visual Grammar*. New York: Princeton Architectural Press.

Lupton, E., & Abbott Miller, J. (1991). *The ABC's of Bauhaus: The Bauhaus and Design Theory*. New York: Herb Lubalin Center of Design and Typography, Cooper Union School of Art.

Lupton, E., & Abbott Miller, J. (2006). *Design Writing Research: Writing on Graphic Design*. London: Phaidon Books.

Margolin, V., & Buchanan, R. (Eds.). (1995). *The Idea of Design: A Design Issues Reader*. Cambridge, MA: MIT Press.

Michel, R. (2007). *Design Research Now: Essays and Selected Projects*. Basel, Switzerland: Birkhäuser Verlag.

Poynor, R. (2003). *No More Rules: Graphic Design and Postmodernism*. London: Laurence King.

Poynor, R. (2001). *Obey the Giant: Life in the Image World*, 2nd edition. Basel, Switzerland: Birkhäuser Verlag.

Rose, G. (2007). *Visual Methodologies: An Introduction to the Interpretation of Visual Materials*. London: SAGE.

Wilde, J., & Wilde, R. (1991). *Visual Literacy: A Conceptual Approach to Solving Graphic Problems*. New York: Watson-Guptill.

Contributing Designers

Alison Barnes
Email: alison.barnes7@gmail.com
Web: alisonbarnesonlineportfolio.tumblr.com

Lucy Brown
Email: lucy@lucybrown.co
Web: www.lucybrown.co

Matt Cooke
Email: matt@ironcreative.com
Web: www.ironcreative.com

Charlotte Knibbs
Email: say@likeyougiveadamn.com
Web: www.likeyougiveadamn.com

Nick Lovegrove
Email: nick.lovegrove@gmail.com
Web: nicklovegrove.co.uk

Dan McCabe
Email: dan@graphicamusing.co.uk
Web: www.graphicamusing.co.uk

Paul McNeil
Email: pm@muirmcneil.com
Web: www.muirmcneil.com

Rob Mowbray
Email: rob_mowbray@432limited.com
Web: http://cargocollective.com/robmowbray
Blog: http://rob-dirtywork.blogspot.co.uk/

Orlagh O'Brien
Email: hello@orlaghobrien.com
Web: www.orlaghobrien.com

Niall O'Shea
Email: hello@nialloshea.com
Web: www.nialloshea.com

Edouard Pecher
Email: ed@tomorrow.works
Web: tomorrow.works

Peter Rüpschl
Email: peter@ruepschl.com
Web: www.ruepschl.com

Colette Sadlier
Email: hello@colettesadlier.com
Web: www.colettesadlier.com

Alex Thornton
Email: alex22362@gmail.com
Web: www.alexeala.net

Location photography front cover and pp. 015, 022–023,
025, 097, 099, 119, 121, 138–139, 141, 145, 147, 169,
171, 191, 193, 195 © Sarah Dryden.
Email: drydensarah@hotmail.com

Index

Index

223

Index

Acknowledgments

We would like to thank the former staff and students in the Postgraduate Graphic Design program at the London College of Communication for their critical contribution to the developments in design thinking outlined in this book. Special thanks must go to the contributing designers, whose work exemplifies many of the ideas explored during our work on graphic design methodologies and practice over the past twenty years. Their contribution to our critical thinking process should not be underestimated.

Russell Bestley

I worked closely with Ian for over twenty years between 1990 and 2013. Our shared vision for a more engaged form of graphic design practice and theory drove our exploration of the subject; our involvement in research, teaching, and learning; and our practical work under the joint name *Visual Research*—as well as our ongoing conversations on innumerable train journeys, flights, and long drives to work with collaborators around the world. We lectured together, taught classes together, gave public presentations together, and over time we settled into a comfortable working relationship, bouncing ideas and trading arguments—often employing barbed comments to subtly pierce any sign of egotism or pretentiousness creeping into each other's line of deliberation.

We agreed on a 50/50 split for all acknowledgements for our work, choosing to rotate authorship credits as Noble & Bestley or Bestley & Noble with each project—a completely democratic meeting of minds and a genuine working partnership. This book is the culmination of our working lives together, though tragically I have had to work on this revised, rewritten, and updated third edition of *Visual Research* alone. This would have been my turn to lead in the credits, but in tribute to Ian I have left the order similar to the first two editions. When we wrote our acknowledgements for the second edition of *Visual Research*, Ian described my highly emotional thanks to friends, family, and my recently departed mother as my "Gwyneth Paltrow Oscar speech"—he chose instead to quote Dee Dee Ramone's acceptance speech at the ceremony to mark the induction of the Ramones into the Rock and Roll Hall of Fame: *"I would like to thank myself, and congratulate myself, and if I could, I would pat myself on the back."* Ian was a huge figure in graphic design, and his sudden and tragic passing in early 2013 left an enormous void in the lives of the many that knew and loved him. I feel proud to have known and worked with such a charismatic, compassionate, and downright bloody funny partner in crime.

http://ian-tribute.studioandrewhoward.com

Sarah Dryden

I would like to thank Russ and Ian for including me in their *Visual Research* journey. *Visual Research* gave me the opportunity to see word, and image, and research methods debated in a contemporary, innovative way. It's not often a photographer is given the freedom to explore key concepts of an author's work—indeed all my professional partnerships are now benchmarked in relation to the Bestley-Noble experience. Many thanks to Pauline and Babs, aka Bestley & Noble.

Visual Research, 3rd edition: Design, Layout, Diagrams, and Illustrations © Russell Bestley and Ian Noble. Photography © Sarah Dryden.